Justice Rising

Justice Rising

The Emerging Biblical Vision

John Heagle

ORBIS BOOKS

Maryknoll, New York 10545

Second Printing, April 2012

Founded in 1970, Orbis Books endeavors to publish works that enlighten the mind, nourish the spirit, and challenge the conscience. The publishing arm of the Maryknoll Fathers & Brothers, Orbis seeks to explore the global dimensions of the Christian faith and mission, to invite dialogue with diverse cultures and religious traditions, and to serve the cause of reconciliation and peace. The books published reflect the views of their authors and do not represent the official position of the Maryknoll Society. To learn more about Maryknoll and Orbis Books, please visit our website at www.maryknollsociety.org.

Library of Congress Cataloging-in-Publication Data

Heagle, John.
    Justice rising : the emerging biblical vision / John Heagle.
        p. cm.
    Includes bibliographical references and index.
    ISBN 978-1-57075-884-3 (pbk.)
    1. Christianity and justice—Catholic Church. 2. Justice—Biblical teaching. I. Title.
    BX1795.J87H43   2010
    220.8'303372—dc22

                                        2010008380

To Archbishop Raymond Hunthausen,
servant of justice, man of peace

Contents

Introduction

The world is on terror alert. We are at war.

This is the description of events that we face daily, from our first cup of coffee in the morning until the late news at night. Terrorism has become so commonplace that we have created ways of measuring its probability. We calibrate it in colors, ranging from green to red. We portray it in categories, moving from low to critical. We employ language that evokes vigilance without intending to provoke panic. But beneath these diverse ways of describing danger, there is a common reality. From India, Pakistan, Yemen, Sri Lanka, and Southeast Asia to Israel, the United Kingdom, Spain, France, and the United States, a pervading atmosphere of *fear* is rising along with the levels of vigilance.

This escalating sense of panic is the defined purpose of terrorism. It is intended to destabilize the collective psyche of the human community and to cripple the quest for peace. Ironically, it is no longer depression but anxiety that has become the leading cause of psychological stress and spiritual fatigue in today's world. Experts tell us that further attacks are inevitable. There will be more sophisticated I.E.D.s and new methods of incursion—on planes, in airports, subways, shopping malls, cyberspace, university campuses, sports arenas, seaports, theater districts, or crowded tourist areas. For many citizens the war against terror has become the focal point of their personal and political awareness. From their perspective this is a struggle not only to protect our way of life but to defend civilization itself.

So why write a book on justice? Why pursue a vision of peacemaking? Increasingly, it seems, these are the last concerns on the minds and hearts of most people. Justice and peace might remain far-off dreams or vague hopes, but for the majority of citizens they are not a

New Normal podcast
suggest we could
to not need it
from ourselves

current priority. We are at war, the media, the politicians, and many religious leaders remind us. This is not a time for idealism or lofty rhetoric. This is a summons to battle.

From the outset, I want to be clear. I believe that we must confront terrorism and our escalating fears surrounding it. Fear is the emotion of human survival. It is the energy of protection that mobilizes the human body and the global community to act decisively. We clearly need this "adrenaline of the spirit" at this time in history.

But there are deeper questions. What is our fear striving to protect? And what lies beneath its vigilance? Fear can easily become a self-defeating response if it is not accompanied by reflection, a spirit of solidarity, and a commitment to overcome the conditions that cause violence in the first place. Being alert and taking defensive action—however vital and necessary—are only first steps. Yes, we need to be vigilant. Of course, we should be informed, responsible, and engaged. But what else is demanded of us? While fear is a necessary response, it cannot be a permanent way of life. Unless we begin to examine the roots of terror, both as an irrational response and as a calculated technique of destruction, we will only increase the levels of mistrust, hatred, and violence in our world.

Embracing the vision of biblical justice and pursuing the way of peace are, I believe, the demanding path that we must walk in the years ahead. Even if these tasks are widely perceived as naïve and tactically ineffective, they are nevertheless close to the heart of Christian discipleship. Given the imminent threat of terrorism, the self-described pragmatists among us have already concluded that the vision of Jesus of Nazareth is unrealistic, otherworldly, and politically inept. In a culture of power-as-domination, this is a reasonable assessment. They are correct. The Jesus we encounter in the Gospels is not interested in power as expediency or politics as usual. However, if this assumption is as widespread as it appears, then we are facing disturbing questions regarding our religious traditions and the systemic roots of violence. Exploring these unsettling questions is the starting point of our journey into justice.

Recently, I was invited to give a presentation on biblical justice at a parish in the Pacific Northwest. Toward the end of our discussion, a university student stood up and spoke with quiet conviction. She told us that her search to make sense of her faith had led her to a painful conclusion. She had come to believe that most religions—including the Judeo-Christian tradition—were no longer credible. I clearly recall her final question: "How can religions that are so immersed in violence speak to us about being just, let alone making peace?"

I believe this young woman's question deserves to be taken seriously. Anyone who has studied the Hebrew and Christian Scriptures is aware that alongside stories of love and salvation there are shocking episodes of vengeance, violence, even holy wars. In our tradition there have been three basic ways of dealing with the "problem of violence." The first is to ignore it, and selectively focus on the love of God and neighbor. The second is to claim it, directly or indirectly, as a justification for the continued use of violence in the name of God. The third is to confront this issue directly, by exploring the critical, historical, and theological evolution of the meaning of biblical justice and peacemaking.

This book builds on the third approach. It confronts the reality of violence in our tradition, but it also explores the dramatic shift in ethical consciousness that leads us beyond retributive justice toward restorative and transformative justice. The violence that is described in the Bible—and in the sacred writings of other religions, including Islam—is frighteningly real. We cannot deny it or pretend that it isn't there. Nor can we use the violent scriptural narratives as a moral justification for our reliance on war as the primary way of pursuing peace. Instead, we need to recognize that vengeance was an early, primitive form of justice making. Violence was practiced by ancient tribes and early nation states as an understandable, but futile, effort to protect their people and to survive in a precarious world. This does not justify its continued, indiscriminate use in our emerging global community. In the chapters that follow, we explore an evolving ethic that emerges early in the history of God's people, an inspired, slowly dawning consciousness that envisions a different way of achieving safety, of seeking justice, and creating community.

An Evolving Ethic

What is this evolving ethic? It is a slender thread of prophetic consciousness. It moves from the early, more primitive understanding of justice as avenging blood to the gradual emergence of inclusion, compassion, and ultimately the gift of self in the service of reconciliation and peace. This vision has its origins in the Sinai covenant and God's saving act of liberation on behalf of the Hebrew people. It is likewise

seen in the changing role of the *go'el,* the designated protector of
community, the figure who, from earliest times, is called to maintain
the safety of tribal life. It is further developed in the prophets, more
explicitly envisioned in the mysterious figure of the *'ebed Yahweh* (servant of the Lord) in Isaiah, and finally brought to fulfillment, for those
of us who claim to be Christian, in the life and ministry, the dying and
rising of Jesus of Nazareth.

In the Hebrew writings, justice is often pictured as coming down
from God: "Shower, O heavens, from above, and let the skies rain
down righteousness" (Isa 45:8).[1] Or the familiar words of Amos: "Let
justice roll down like waters, and righteousness like an ever-flowing
stream" (Amos 5:24). These metaphors remind us of God's initiative
in seeking to protect the poor and the vulnerable. But the river of
justice is not a wandering stream. It flows with purpose and direction. The flood of divine justice is intended to pour into our hearts. It
is a rain that is meant to soak into the ground of our being, a torrent
that transforms our lives to become a river of righteousness. Isaiah's
poetry articulates this clearly:

> For as the rain and snow come down from heaven,
>   and do not return there until they have watered
>   the earth,
> making it bring forth and sprout,
>   giving seed to the sower and bread to the eater,
> so shall my word be that goes out from my mouth;
>   it shall not return to me empty,
> but it shall accomplish that which I purpose,
>   and succeed in the thing for which I sent it.
>   (Isa 55:10-11)

God's seeking care is rain for our drought, a soaking consolation
in our desert—*and* a challenge to our self-preoccupation and fear of
the other. It is intended to become, in the words of Jesus, "a spring of
water gushing up to eternal life" (John 4:14). This is the wellspring of
justice that I explore in this book—the emergence of God's solidarity
in human relationships. *This is justice rising.*

Through the gradual emergence of ethical awareness, the people
of God were invited to make a long inward journey, a world-altering
change in their way of thinking. They were challenged to give up
the practice of taking other people's blood in a desperate search for

protection, and instead to become willing to give their own lives in order to restore relationships and create authentic *shalom*. This is nothing less than a God-initiated transformation. It is far beyond our usual human reactions to fear or danger—so far beyond them, that perhaps it would be more correct to describe this as an ethical *revolution*, a leap of moral consciousness, a commitment that moves us beyond conventional forms of citizenship and religion.

DOES RELIGION HAVE A ROLE?

Martin Luther King reminds us that "the arc of the moral universe is long, but it bends toward justice" (sermon at the National Cathedral, March 31, 1968). In these pages, we follow this arc of spiritual consciousness and its implications for us as individuals, for our communities of faith, and ultimately for our human institutions. This is a book about changing our ways of thinking. And choosing. And relating. And living. It is an invitation to reimagine what it means to be human *and* just in our wounded, weary world. Change is inevitable, but following a responsible path is still an option and becoming ever more dependent on the way we think and choose. Our scientists will continue to develop faster and more efficient tools of information. The challenge is whether we can turn this information into wisdom and authentic communication—into a listening spirit, a genuine dialogue between persons and nations.

If changing our ways of thinking is crucial, there is another, equally urgent question. What role can religion play in shaping this emerging vision? Will religious traditions continue to be a source of division and violent conflict, or will they move past their focus on doctrinal orthodoxy and reclaim their role as a spiritual energy for compassion and healing, a compelling force calling us to the tasks of justice and the works of peace?

For most people in Europe and the United States, the term "terrorism" immediately evokes images of Muslim extremists blowing themselves up to destroy people whose way of life they abhor. Currently, there is a fierce debate among political commentators and religious scholars as to whether Islam and the Qur'an are inherently violent.[2] This is not surprising, since in times of crisis we tend toward polarized ways of thinking. Creating stereotypes is a direct outcome of this fear-based approach to life. We conveniently forget that the

Muslim world is as diverse and multifaceted as Christianity and Judaism. There are conflicting versions of Islam, just as there are differing
interpretations of the Christian gospel or contemporary Jewish faith.
Most Christians would be outraged if other world religions equated
our ethical practices with the Ku Klux Klan, even though their members claim to be Christian. Similarly, it is unfair to identify the entire
Muslim world with the Taliban, Al-Qaeda, or the extremists who
planned and carried out 9/11.

That being said, it is clear that Muslims face a challenge similar to
that of Christians and other religious traditions. The word "Islam" is a
verbal noun that, in its Arabic etymology, means "submission to God."
Integral to this spirituality is the willingness to reach out to the poor
and to seek harmony between peoples. Thus, the Muslim community is
challenged—as are we—to reclaim the central vision of justice in their
tradition and to understand their religion as an ethical commitment to
human dignity, respect, and the responsibility of pursuing peace.

The focus of these chapters is on the evolution of justice in the
Judeo-Christian tradition. But I believe there is a similar task facing the scholars of the Qur'an, as well as ordinary Muslim believers,
namely, the call to renew their spiritual vision and to reclaim restorative justice as central to their religious and political practice. In brief,
we all share a common call to ongoing renewal and conversion.

The first recorded words of Jesus in the Gospel are a summons
to change. "The time is fulfilled, and the kingdom of God has come
near; repent, and believe in the good news" (Mark 1:15). The Greek
verb (*metanoeite*) is translated in diverse ways, most often as "repent"
or "be converted." But it literally means "to change your mind," or to
alter one's way of seeing and interpreting life. Jesus is not speaking of
exploring rational alternatives in a detached, scientific manner. Nor is
he inviting us to grovel in moral guilt. Rather, he is challenging each
of us to change our hearts—our attitudes, our assumptions, and our
stance before life and people.

In the end, the need to change goes beyond culture, politics, and
religious institutions. It confronts human persons at the core of their
being. "The journey of a thousand miles," in the familiar words of
Lao Tzu, "begins with one step." This first step is one that each of us
must make. No one else can make this choice for us. Without our personal commitment, it will not be a shared journey, a common cause.
It is convenient to blame institutions and systems for their failure to
respond to crises. But institutions are simply the outcome of individ-

or from Aramaic
return to center
to Unity

uals in community who are striving to create structures of growth and stability. Politics and culture are the self writ large, as it recognizes and responds to the web of creation. It is the self in relationship— with God, with our sisters and brothers, but also with our mother, the earth. What form of personal transformation or radical conversion is required of each of us to help change the systems that create our communal selves? How do we move further ahead in the task of changing our minds and hearts?

THE PURPOSE AND APPROACH OF THIS BOOK

This book addresses these vital questions by exploring the meaning and evolution of biblical justice and its challenge for contemporary faith communities. It also describes the need for a personal and communal conversion that flows from this vision and its implications for our lives. Although this study deals with biblical scholarship and history, it is my hope to make these ideas accessible, challenging, and potentially life-changing.

I hope to accomplish three goals in these pages. The first is to outline the remarkable evolution of what it means, from a biblical perspective, to "do justice" and to create peace. This is no small task, since many people still fuse (or con-fuse) justice with their current understanding of civil justice. Biblical justice, as it emerges in our sacred story, is far more demanding than our popular understanding of the rule of law. It calls us to be responsible citizens, yes, but more than that, it calls us to gospel *metanoia*—a more radical change of mind and heart in the service of the reign of God.

The second goal is to relate these biblical themes to our religious institutions. Our sacred traditions contain not only doctrines, but also unspoken assumptions and attitudes about violence, war, punishment, global economies, and the practice of advocacy for the poor. In my Catholic tradition there is a central emphasis on social justice as a way of making the gospel present in the world. The Second Vatican Council reaffirmed this commitment to create peace by working for authentic justice. The 1971 Synod of Bishops issued a document entitled *Justice in the World*, in which they stated: "Action on behalf of justice and participation in the transformation of the world fully appear to us as a *constitutive dimension of preaching the Gospel*, or in other words, of the Church's mission for the redemption of the human race and its liberation from every oppressive situation."[3] These are clear, unambiguous words that articulate our contemporary ecclesial vision. For the most part, however, this vision, along with the broader teachings on social justice and their implementation, continues to be the Church's best kept secret.

Finally, I want to apply this evolving ethic of justice to our personal lives, to our immediate circle of relationships, and to the communities in which we live. The vision of justice that unfolded over thousands of years in the Judeo-Christian tradition must somehow come to birth in each of us. This is simply another way of describing the path of Christian discipleship. This third focus addresses the call to spiritual growth—perhaps more correctly, personal transformation—in each of our lives, as we try, with God's grace, to internalize and to live the story that we have inherited. Through concrete examples related to contemporary life, we will explore our call to move from vengeance to healing, from retribution to restoration, from exclusion to inclusion, from the clenched fist to an open hand.

1

Encountering a God of Liberation

Justice in an Evolving Cosmos

From the beginning till now the entire creation, as we know, has been groaning in one great act of giving birth.
                                                    —Romans 8:22 (JB)

Our awakening is an awakening of God and our rising is God's rising.
                            —John of the Cross, *The Living Flame of Love*

In an essay written in 1920, the Jesuit scientist and mystic Pierre Teilhard de Chardin describes two different ways of viewing the cosmos and our relationship to it.[1] He invites us to picture the universe as a vast ocean, and to see ourselves as passengers on a small raft. From the deck of our vessel, we gaze toward the horizon and pose the questions that human beings have always asked. Why are we here? Are we going anywhere? Is there an underlying direction for the universe? Or are we simply adrift on a sea of oblivion?

One group of people scans the horizon and reports that nothing is happening. We are not moving; we are only drifting. There is no direction, no destiny, and no sign of promise. This group represents the "immobilists," who cling to the status quo and do not believe in an evolving universe.

But there is another group on the raft who also search the sea and the sky. They are driven by a spirit of adventure, a hunger for meaning. As they scan the stars, they stand against the night of despair. They study the movement of the waves and listen to the sound of the night wind. They watch the world with the eyes of hope. So they are not surprised to hear a shout from the lookout: "We are *moving!*" This group represents those who believe that life is a dynamic unfolding and that we human beings are called to share in this growth, perhaps even to help shape it.

CREATION AND JUSTICE: AN EMERGING JOURNEY

In Teilhard's essay, the metaphor of passengers on a raft serves as a starting point for a reflection on evolution and human conscious-ness. It also gives us a striking image for the emerging understand-ing of justice in the global community. From the earliest footprints of human history there is evidence that the powerful have exploited the more vulnerable members of the human family. Today's "immobil-ists" want us to believe that this is the way human beings have always been, that this is how they are, and that this is how they will always be. Regrettably, it appears as though this first group—who claim the high ground of moral realism and political practicality—are accurate in their appraisal of human nature. There is abundant evidence to support their argument. Violence and injustice continue to spiral out of control; the best intentions and efforts of the global community appear to be futile.

But there is another band of seekers who—like the second group on the raft—believe in the future and in our responsibility to help shape it. They are often dismissed as idealists or dreamers. In reality, however, they are courageous prophets who are willing to test their convictions in the turbulent seas of life and in the rocky terrain of his-tory. Given today's escalating violence, they may well be the ultimate realists, the most practical people of all, because they are committed to working for the earth's survival through human responsibility in community. They look with the eyes of hope and walk with the heart of faith. They take seriously their call to work for the reign of God and its quiet, resilient flowering in our struggling world. They have the audacity to claim the work of justice as the premier path toward peace. They hear the call to personal conversion and the gospel sum-mons to hunger for justice and to work for peace. In the face of grow-ing oppression, violence, and polarization, they are willing to commit their lives to the task of shaping the future together.

What vision sustains their hope? I believe it is the experience of a God who is not only a creator but a *liberator*. It is the spirit of the holy in the unfolding cosmos and in the human community that is leading us toward greater consciousness, responsibility, and service. In the unfinished symphony that is creation, the "mighty wind of God" continues to blow across our moral chaos and our systems of exploitation to bring forth a new order, to summon authentic human aspirations, to stir the dark waters into life. This, in turn, is the enduring task which we humans have the privilege of claiming as well.

Where do we find the roots of this passion for justice? Our obvious source is the Judeo-Christian tradition and its sacred writings. But it is no easy task to uncover the emergence of restorative justice in the story of salvation. The Jewish and Christian scriptures are too complex, too rich, and too diverse to be reduced to one theme. The word of God is like a great tapestry in which are woven together the call and response, the events and encounters of God and humanity. And yet there is one pattern that appears in all parts of this immense fabric. It is so recurrent, so central that it becomes an integral feature of the whole. It underlies all the other themes and gives them direction and unity. In a word, it is the theme of *journey*.

EVOLUTION AS LIBERATION

It is not just any voyage that we share. This is a journey toward deeper and more expansive life. Specifically, it is a passage toward *liberation*. We are part of a universe that is still coming alive, still unfolding in hope. The J. B. Phillips translation of the Christian Scriptures says it well: "The whole creation is on tiptoe to see the wonderful sight of the sons [and daughters] of God coming into their own" (Rom 8:19).

What would it imply for our communities of faith "to come into their own"? What would it mean for each of us, as members of the human race, to live out the truth of our calling? There is indeed an emerging, shared intuition that creation is standing on tiptoe, straining to see in what direction the human community will choose to walk. It is as though we are summoned to a new moment of shared responsibility, poised at the edge of vast possibilities. A persistent inwardness stirs in our consciousness, like a new dawn breaking through the morning clouds, a promise waiting to be realized. There are things hidden since the beginning of time that are still being revealed, secrets of the reign of God to be embodied, creative energies waiting to be set free. The question is whether we will hear this invitation. Have cre-

ation and God's good earth unfolded through 13.7 billion years only to
end in our communal failure to choose life? Or will we make the next
step in the journey toward authentic freedom?

Before we pursue these questions further, there is an important
clarification to be made. When I speak of liberation, I am not describing the ancient and illusory longing to be delivered from the human
condition. This is not a case of being released from the secular to
the spiritual, from flesh to spirit, from our bodies to Plato's "eternal
forms." We are not seeking an escape hatch from history. If anything,
this is a call to leap into the chaotic, spinning, eruptive energy of matter. "Remember that you are dust and unto dust you shall return" (cf.
Gen 3:19), as the ancient ritual of Ash Wednesday reminds us. True
enough. We are indeed fragile, passing creatures, like the grass that is
here today only to wither and fade tomorrow (Isa 40:6-8). But there
is more, much more. We are created from cosmic dust, but—in the
colorful images of Scripture—it is dust breathed into by the creator of
the universe (Gen 2:7). Remember that you are *star* dust, we can confidently assert, and the blossoming of billions of years of an unfolding
mystery. Thus, we are describing liberation not as a flight from life but
as an embrace of matter, mortality, and mystery. We are speaking of
the call to be an integral part of the unfinished symphony of creation.

What is this deeper pattern of liberation? It is an emergence from
any form of bondage or exploitation. In human history it involves the
long struggle to become free from oppression and destructive violence. The first creation story of Genesis opens with the *ruah 'elohim*—
the wind, breath, or spirit of God—moving across the face of chaos to
create the stunning beauty of the cosmos. It is the Bible's first account
of God's liberating role. Later, the exodus and its passage from slavery
to freedom become the central metaphor of Israel's relationship with
God. For Christians, the "passing over" of Jesus through his death to
new life is the core symbol of our salvation. The last of the Christian
Scriptures, the Book of Revelation, closes with the early community
longing with radiant hope for the coming of the risen Christ—the
final liberation into the beloved community.

Notice that this concept of liberating justice is more expansive than
what we have, in the past, referred to as "salvation history." We are
speaking of a mystery that is unfolding in all of creation, not just with
human beings. This is what Loren Eiseley describes as the "immense
journey" of creation[2]—the unfolding of the universe through the evolution of energy, matter, biological life, and human consciousness. In

this sense, the entire 13.7 billion years of this universe is salvation history. Liberation has been at work for all these billions of years. Evolution is itself a transformative passage—an exodus—from less complex forms of life to more developed forms. Its path is clearly toward deeper awareness and reflective consciousness, for it flowers in the gift of intentional freedom—the challenge of taking responsibility for the care of the earth and of being compassionate toward our sisters and brothers. It is a passing over from (apparently) inert being to becoming vibrantly alive, from being bound by externality to blossoming into inwardness and the surprise of creative imagination.

The contemporary theologian and cosmologist John Haught describes this parallel between our faith tradition and the way that we have come to view the journey of the universe.[3] The first image that should come to mind when we read or hear the word of God, he maintains, is *liberation*:

> Biblical religion is all about renewal, promise, and liberation. And that seemed to me to be enough of a theological framework on which to plant my interest in evolution as well. I view evolution not just in terms of biology but in terms of the development of the whole universe from the monotony of radiation to the complexity of the human brain and the emergence of civilization and culture. And when you look at it in that sweeping way, you see that the universe is a pretty interesting place, and it's been interested in bringing about new being, more being, more intense being, from the very beginning.[4]

To bring about "new being, more being, and more intense being" in the world: Isn't this another way of speaking about the work of justice? Renewal, promise, liberation: Are not these words that describe the task of justice making? The first step toward reimaging the meaning of biblical justice as a path toward peace requires that we embark on this more expansive worldview. It challenges us to open our horizons, to take the wide-angle view that Teilhard, Haught, Thomas Berry, Brian Swimme, and other cosmologists are inviting us to embrace today.

Let us not be mistaken. To expand the screen of our human consciousness will threaten many of our familiar assumptions. From the outset, it invites us to link our everyday notions of fairness, as well as the biblical accounts of justice, to the liberating journey that is unfolding everywhere in the universe. It also challenges us to reenvision the origins and reach of the human story. What does it mean to speak of "human history"? When does it begin? How do we depict it? In our myopic, self-focused way of thinking we have tended to identify our story from a narrow time line. Most traditional historians consider human history to begin approximately ten to twelve thousand years ago with the advent of agriculture and primitive forms of record keeping. It's as if we are saying that nothing counted before we developed the tools to record it.

The contemporary sciences of paleontology and anthropology remind us that this perspective is too restricted. Its time line is incomplete, its perspective too anthropocentric. We are not a species apart from the rest of our developing universe. Human history is part of the larger 13.7 billion years of cosmic evolution. Seen from this perspective, contemporary theologians are inviting us to view human evolution itself in terms of "deep time."[5] From this more spacious point of view we can detect the appearance of "proto-humans" as early as seven million years ago. At crucial turning points the early, developing human brain was able—through grace and creative instinct—to maintain a vital bond with the rest of the earth community and at the same time to evolve in its ability to develop tools, to expand its connection to the earth, and to search out new horizons. It is only in the last ten thousand years that we have become so destructive. In the succeeding chapters, we will explore the complex and challenging reasons for this turn toward violence. For now it is enough to locate the search for justice and peace in a wider context and to affirm our solidarity with the rest of creation.

LIVING THE GREAT STORY

The stars and those who watch them tell us that our universe is immense beyond all measuring. In the same way, those who study the earth and its life remind us that our history began billions of years before we began to write it down. And yet, for the most part, we earthlings continue to tell ourselves a truncated version of a boundless story. Science has long given us information to stretch our minds, but it is only recently that this knowledge has begun to fire our imaginations and expand our hearts. It is only in the last half-century, for instance, that we have begun to speak of this immensity and its history as an experiential truth that shapes our vision and our spirituality. We are the first generations of human beings to share a common creation story. "Every living being of the Earth is cousin to every other living being. Even beyond the realm of the living we have a common origin in the primordial Flaring Forth of the energies from which the universe in all its aspects is derived."[6]

Most of us have experiences that enlarge our lives and unite us with this wider story. Sometimes this occurs when we encounter what psychologists refer to as "peak experiences"—altered states of consciousness that disrupt our usual way of looking at life. Often these turning points or moments of insight go unnamed, even unnoticed. All the same, they reveal the quiet work of the Spirit moving in our lives, urging us forward in the quest for meaning.

I recall one such experience from my youth. As a boy growing up on a dairy farm in Wisconsin, I had the privilege—without fully appreciating it at the time—of being close to the earth and the rhythm of the seasons. I remember a summer evening, sitting on our hay wagon as twilight turned to night and watching the panoply of stars silently appear. From the nearby woods I could hear the song of a whippoorwill. I watched the moon rise over the eastern hills and bathe the earth with its radiance. In that moment, no one needed to explain that we live in an expansive, spacious cosmos. Nor did I need to look up evolution in the encyclopedia. I was enveloped by these living truths. I saw them with my eyes. I heard them in my breath. I felt them in my body.

Later, as an adult, I recall the transformation of our horizons that accompanied the space voyages to the moon. The crew of the Apollo 8—Frank Borman, James Lovell, and William Anders—were the first humans to leave earth orbit and enter lunar orbit. On Christmas Eve, 1968, along with a reading from Genesis and greetings "to all of you on the good earth," they sent back the historic photo of "Earthrise" over the lunar landscape. Only six months later, on July 20, 1969, the Apollo 11 crew landed on the moon and Neil Armstrong became the first human to walk on the lunar surface. That night I stood on the bluffs above the Mississippi River with a small group of friends, watching the night sky in wonder. It truly was "a giant leap" for humankind.

Is this simply a victory for scientific technology, or is there a deeper significance? Just as important, what does it have to do with reimaging biblical justice? The voyage to the moon is a metaphor for the adventure of the human spirit. It isn't just that our technology was successful, or that our astronauts were more skilled, or that we won the race to the moon. This event is larger than politics, and it exceeds the bounds of science. It is nothing less than a breakthrough to a new awareness as a human community. When we viewed the first earthrise from the other side of the moon, it wasn't just another photograph. It was a moment of collective insight, an encounter with "holy communion," a shared mystical moment. This historic footage is literally a new window on our world. The familiar proverb is proven true in this instance. One picture is worth a thousand words—perhaps many libraries of words.

Long before Copernicus and Galileo, we had been told that we were not the center of the universe. But for the most part, psychologically, culturally, and spiritually we continued to assume an earlier anthropocentric perspective. Heaven is up there; hell is somewhere beneath us. The sun rises in the east and sets in the west; the constellations and the stars circle silently around us as seasons come and go. Whatever science might tell us about the universe, we seemed content to maintain this tidy, more familiar view of the world.

The photo of the earthrise changed all that. Consider the ways that this picture has impacted our perspective, even our language. We went to the heavens only to behold the earth itself as a "heavenly body." After viewing this image, we discovered that it is no longer possible to understand ourselves as the "wide, wide world" of the 1940s newsreels. We speak today of the "blue planet" against the dark horizon of deep space. We describe ourselves as living on "spaceship earth." In a similar way, this new horizon is profoundly reshaping our understanding of the human community. From space there are no national borders or lines of battle, no denominational or doctrinal boundaries, only a stunningly beautiful planet pulsating with life, a dwelling place of community and promise.

Ironically, this breakthrough to a new awareness has brought more anxiety than hope. It is no accident that over the last decades there has been a flood of books, films, and religious rhetoric surrounding the coming "end of the world." This premonition is not untrue, it is just incorrectly interpreted. Psychologically and spiritually, the photograph of the earthrise tells us—in ways that scientific data cannot—that the world as we have known it has indeed come to an end. We can no longer picture our planet as the center of the universe, or the earth as separate from the heavens, or matter divided off from the world of spirit. But new horizons also bring fresh waves of uncertainty, as is evidenced in the widespread sense of the apocalyptic that envelops our age. Perhaps this is related to the death and

resurrection of human meaning in our time. When the primal metaphors for meaning are transformed, the result more often than not is
fear. Joseph Campbell points out that our symbols are like compasses:
"One point is in a fixed place but the other moves to the unknown. The
fear of the unknown, this free fall into the future, can be detected all
around us. But we live in the stars and we are finally moved by awe to
our greatest adventures."[7]

To embark on "our greatest adventures" is both exciting and terrifying; it means that we are faced with two major psychic shifts. First,
we need to leave behind our familiar view of the world; and, second,
we are summoned to welcome and enlarge our sense of communion
with the rest of creation. Until now, the notion of an expanding universe has been primarily a scientific, rational hypothesis. The religious
imagination needs to bridge the gulf between science and faith that
has occurred since the Enlightenment. We are only beginning to inte-
grate recent scientific knowledge with the deeper life of the psyche.
We have not yet found the symbols—the sacred *mythos*—that are
integral to our spiritual vision and the celebration of the holy. We
have not yet begun to face the full implications of this transformation
for our religious traditions or our emerging global political structures.

And yet there are already creative stirrings. In the epigraph at the
beginning of this chapter, St. Paul reminds us that "all of creation . . .
is groaning in one great act of giving birth." Then he adds that "we
too groan inwardly" (Rom 8:23 [JB]). This is an apt metaphor for the
struggle and conflict, the confusion and promise that accompany a
time of radical change. We can hear the "groaning" in the widespread
fundamentalist resistance to a renewed vision of the human project.
On the other hand, the language that expresses this shift is ultimately
hopeful. It speaks of green revolutions and bread for the world, of
rainbow coalitions and the axis of equality, of global efforts to fight
poverty and disease, of habitats for humanity, of movements to sustain the education of women and children, and of collaborative efforts
to combat international violence.

EMBRACING HISTORICAL CONSCIOUSNESS

If the first task is to view our world in a more expansive way, the second is to reimagine our relationship to the arc of history. For billions
of years the spirit of God has been at work in the universe bringing

forth new, intriguing manifestations of energy and matter. These in turn produced ever more complex, intricate forms of life. Approximately seven million years ago, the first stirrings of reflective self-consciousness began to appear in proto-humans. At a certain critical threshold these early forms of interiority leapt beyond instinct and sensory awareness and blossomed into self-consciousness: the capacity to think, to wonder, to love, to confront the mystery of death, to make intentional choices, and to become aware of moral responsibility. From that point on, human beings became what Teilhard de Chardin describes as the "arrow" or leading edge of evolution. In the human community evolution has become conscious of itself. We walk on the good earth aware of time. Each morning we awake to the promise—and the task—of the future.

Today we speak of this complex phenomenon as "historical consciousness." This implies that the future is no longer something that merely happens to us. Rather, we are in some way responsible for helping to shape it. In earlier times the world was often viewed from a static perspective, as in Shakespeare's memorable phrase "All the world's a stage, and all the men and women merely players." Some aspects of our religious heritage tended to reinforce this fixed assumption by diminishing the value of the earth and its history. Our goal, according to this otherworldly perspective, is to leave the earth behind for heaven. Our task is to save our souls, not to build the earth or to contribute to the human community. There may be some who still cling to this escapist spirituality, but in our time we are increasingly challenged to become responsible participants in history. The world is no longer just a stage, a prearranged scene for pilgrims in transit. As human persons, we are more than players, more than mere observers or bystanders. Like it or not, each of us has some part in writing the next act of this real-life story.

We may not have time on our hands, but we have history on our shoulders.

Becoming Authentically Other-Centered

For some people this emphasis on our personal role in shaping history suggests spiritual pride, even arrogance. In reality, however, it is a call to deeper responsibility and generosity. It implies a willingness to commit ourselves to the well-being of others, to discover a world that is larger than our ego. If the primal pattern of creation is a journey of liberation, then it is less about "me" and more about "us." Moving beyond our narrow egos to respect and care for the other is the core spiritual vision of most religious traditions. Each of us, in turn, is challenged to make this personal voyage from our self-centered concerns toward compassion and solidarity. Like the ancient Israelites, each of us is called out of bondage and thrust into the desert to discover that our mission is greater than ourselves.

We live in an increasingly anxiety-ridden world, so much so that for many people each day is a matter of physical and emotional survival. For those who face daily trauma, stress, or a lack of resources, this is an understandable mode of coping. In Abraham Maslow's hierarchy of basic needs, it is clear that we cannot grow toward higher forms of self-actualization unless our basic needs are met. In order to flourish as a human person we require sufficient food, shelter, and clothing, along with a reasonable amount of physical and emotional safety. Self-care is essential to human growth. Thus, while it is true that the great commandment names loving God and others as the first priority, there is also that final phrase: "as you love yourself." Love of self is the last mentioned, but it is integral to engaging the other two tasks. Perhaps this is why flight attendants routinely tell us that in case of an unexpected emergency, we should put on our own oxygen mask first and then care for others around us. In other words, being concerned about ourselves doesn't necessarily mean that we are selfish; it simply implies that we are responsible. Human development involves coming to know ourselves, our gifts and limitations, and claiming our uniqueness in the world.

Some level of self-focus is a normal part of growing up, especially during our adolescent years. The hope is that we will grow through and beyond our self-centered world to become more mature in our concern for our family, our circle of friends and neighbors, our fellow believers, and ultimately our sisters and brothers in the wider human community. At a certain point in our maturing process, we recognize that life is ultimately nourished and enlarged by relationships. We understand that we are summoned to service and other-centered care. For some of us this flows from our formative background in our family and the matrix of our faith. For others it is triggered by leaving home, falling in love, a mystical encounter with the holy, or a life crisis that leaves us suddenly vulnerable and aware of our radical interdependence.

This is a gifted breakthrough in our life journey. We have finally come to realize, in the words of Joseph Campbell that "self-preservation is only the second law of life. *The first law is that you and the other are one.*"[8]

2

Turning Dreams to Ashes

The Reality of War and Violence

*Never shall I forget those moments that murdered my God and my
soul and turned my dreams to ashes.*

—Elie Wiesel

No heaven can justify Auschwitz.

—Dorothee Soelle

Shortly after the U.S. Holocaust Memorial Museum opened in 1993, I
had the privilege of spending a few hours there on a rain-soaked afternoon in autumn. I recall it now not as an adventure in tourism, but
as a pilgrimage into the unspeakable anguish of human suffering. Of
all the bleak scenes, I am haunted especially by the memory of a rail
car that contained hundreds, even thousands of discarded shoes—the
last, silent witness to the millions of Jewish men, women, and children, young and old, who died in the gas chambers.

In the third floor tower room of the permanent exhibition, there
is a row of fence posts from Auschwitz. Displayed next to them are
these words from Elie Wiesel's book *Night*:

> Never shall I forget that night, the first night in camp that
> turned my life into one long night seven times sealed.
> Never shall I forget that smoke.
> Never shall I forget the small faces of the children whose
> bodies I saw transformed into smoke under a silent
> sky.

Never shall I forget those flames that consumed my
    faith forever.
Never shall I forget the nocturnal silence that deprived
    me for all eternity of the desire to live.
Never shall I forget those moments that murdered my
    God and my soul and turned my dreams to ashes.
Never shall I forget those things, even were I
    condemned to live
as long as God Himself.
Never.[1]

Do Not Forget

I shall never forget. Wiesel's words reflect the horror that the victims of
the Holocaust encountered in their lives and that the survivors still carry
in their memory. In the face of unspeakable violence, his words are a cry
against the night, a lament of loss and rage. Among other things, he is
reminding us that the first step in confronting violence is *awareness*—
remaining attentive to life even in the midst of brutality. The work of
justice begins by choosing not to forget. Similarly, the task of peacemaking is sustained by the refusal to drift into collective amnesia.

Do not forget. This is the recurring mandate of the Hebrew Scriptures and the ancient prophets. Do not forget the orphan, the widow,
and the stranger. Do not forget the covenant call to free the oppressed.
Do not forget the God who has been your liberator and your redeemer.
The other side of forgetting is the conscious choice to "keep in mind"
our stories, to carry in our awareness both the pain and the promise
of our lives. "Remember," Moses tells his fellow Israelites, "this day on
which you came out of Egypt, out of the house of slavery, because the
LORD brought you out from there by strength of hand" (Exod 13:3).
"Remember the Lord in a distant land," Jeremiah exhorts the exiles,
"and let Jerusalem come into your mind" (Jer 51:50). "Do this in memory of me," Jesus tells us as he breaks the bread of his life and shares
the blood of his service. "Remember, I am with you always," the risen
Christ tells his disciples and all of us, his future believers (Matt 28:20).

Elie Wiesel and those who endured the hell of the Holocaust will
never forget.

What about the rest of us? We *do* forget, do we not? Not intentionally, not with malice, not because we don't care, not because

we lack compassion, concern, or interest, but because we are over-whelmed with the challenges of our lives. We are distracted, anxious, and obsessed with personal concerns. We suffer from psychic jetlag, a numbing in our souls. We are concerned about our families in chal-lenging economic times. We worry about our jobs, our security, and whether or not we will be able to retire. We are anxious about our health and our vulnerability to cancer, strokes, heart attacks, or rogue viruses. Some of us may even have mundane ways of forgetting—we are preoccupied with famous people, sports heroes, political pundits, or culture wars.

In his familiar phrase, T.S. Eliot tells us that "humankind cannot bear very much reality." This is a poetic way of saying that each of us can become paralyzed by the brittle edges of life, its banality and its losses. It is a sober reminder of the way in which unforeseen circum-stances can shatter our dreams, our health, and our relationships. It is also a way of describing what psychologists call "defense mecha-nisms"—those largely unconscious processes in our psyches (such as repression, denial, and compartmentalization) that enable us to pro-tect ourselves from the raw flow of everyday experience, especially when it becomes emotionally threatening.

Repression, denial, and compartmentalization are, each in its own way, tools of forgetting. They help us survive by practicing a form of subconscious amnesia. In this context, there are two forms of forget-ting that I want to explore. The first takes place with persons who have been through severe trauma. In order to continue on with life, their consciousness must dissociate—which is to say that their psyche lit-erally goes somewhere else, so that they don't spin out of control or completely lose touch with reality. This process of "psychic leaving" is necessary and even healthy for individuals who have undergone a major trauma. In time they are usually able to reconnect to this pain and, in the best of circumstances, to heal from it. It is a rare individ-ual who, like Wiesel, is able to stay present to the trauma and choose awareness in the face of overwhelming suffering.

But there is also another kind of dissociation. This form takes place in people who are not necessarily directly affected by the trauma. It can also occur in individuals or communities who observe or even participate in a violent event or atrocity. Today this type of psychic numbing has become so common that it has been given a psychologi-cal name. It is referred to as the "bystander syndrome." In this case, it is not repression for the sake of survival but a form of collective amnesia that shields individuals and sometimes entire communities from the uncomfortable truth, the horror that is going on around them. For the collective consciousness of a nation it can easily become a tool for ignoring the truth or evading responsibility.

HUMAN VIOLENCE: A GRIM REALITY

The power of visualization is sometimes more persuasive than a mountain of data. So, for a moment, I invite you to imagine the unexpected arrival of friendly aliens from another part of our galaxy. They are, of course, immediately met with a phalanx of TV cameras and reporters. Soon after, experts in linguistics are brought in to establish a means of communication. Our intergalactic visitors are then asked a series of questions: From what part of the universe do you come? What is the level of your scientific knowledge? What kind of language do you speak? What is the nature of your culture, your moral values, your sexual practices, and your religious beliefs? Finally, our visitors take the opportunity to ask us a question: And what about *you*, what is your history on this planet?

How would we respond? What story would we tell about our journey on this earth? Certainly, one version would speak of the rise of civilization, the development of tools, science, technology, writing, music, art, religious institutions, and our exploration of space. Another perspective would tell the story of escalating conflict, wars, injustice, systemic oppression, and brutality. Obviously both versions have a legitimate claim to truth. The difficulty is combining the apparent tensions and contradictions of each account into a single narrative. It is often easier for us to affirm the successes of humankind than to acknowledge our destructive side.

But this much is clear. Elie Wiesel and others like him make a legitimate, urgent plea: *do not forget*. The long night of human violence will only escalate further unless we confront our past with clarity and candor.

What would it be like for us to stand before our history with this kind of realism? If our collective human memory were somehow recorded on film, violence would be the feature story and war would be the background music. Unfortunately our way of explaining this history is simplistic and often irrelevant. Our traditional theology of "original sin" is, at best, a faulty way of understanding the chaos and mystery of human evil. But if we go beyond the flawed rhetoric, it is difficult to argue with the painful reality. We may be created in the image of God, but our history seems to narrate a different story, almost as though we had, from an early time, read the wrong job description.

If we were to tell the truth, we would acknowledge that we are a struggling, often oppressive collection of creatures. There is a fault line through our human story. In Hebrew the word for sin literally means "to miss the mark." To state this in practical terms, we sin when we miss the point of human living—when we become lost in our egos, cut off from one another and from our roots in God. Eckhart Tolle describes the long-term symptoms of this collective state of brokenness:

> If the history of humanity were the clinical case history of a single human being, the diagnosis would have to be: chronic paranoid delusions, a pathological propensity to commit murder and acts of extreme violence and cruelty against his perceived "enemies"—his own unconsciousness projected outward. Criminally insane, with a few brief lucid intervals.[2]

For many of us this is an overly pessimistic judgment on our human journey. But perhaps it is more realistic than we are willing to admit. Most of us have grown so accustomed to bloodshed that we think of it as a given, a normal part of the human condition. How can we break through this dangerous illusion? It will not help to anesthetize our minds or pretend that all is well. Nor will we be motivated to change if we become so focused on the oppressive side of human history that we cannot visualize an alternate way of living. We need to have both a sober realism about violence and, at the same time, a hope that is grounded in action, a firm commitment to work toward the conditions that make for peace.

ESCALATING VIOLENCE

Maintaining the creative tension between realism and authentic hope begins by reflecting on our own stories, by choosing to see ourselves not as bystanders to history but as participants. If we can locate our place in this story, it is no longer a distant narrative leaving us with dates, facts, and abstractions. It becomes instead a threshold into the lived truth of our humanity and ultimately a summons to action. Remembering implies that we are willing to live with conscious intentionality and to carry the consequences of our history. In this way, remembering becomes an act of courage in a world of cultural amnesia.

Like most other human beings, I was born into an age of violence. I didn't understand this at the time, of course. I grew up assuming that my experience was "normal." It was only when I studied modern history in high school that I was challenged to view my life and that of my contemporaries from a more sobering perspective. I learned that when I was less than a year old—on the night of November 9, 1938—the world was spiraling downward toward unimaginable evil, a fracturing of nations and a shattering of human lives. We remember it now as *Kristallnacht* or the "Night of Broken Glass" in Nazi Germany. During those hours of darkness, ninety-one Jewish people were murdered and somewhere between twenty-five and thirty thousand were arrested and deported to concentration camps. More than two hundred synagogues and thousands of Jewish businesses and homes were ransacked or destroyed. Historians today describe this as the beginning of the so-called Final Solution—the systematic effort by the Nazi leaders to eradicate European Jews. And on the wider screen of history it became what we know today as "genocide."

Auschwitz. Buchenwald. Dachau. Bataan. Hiroshima. Nagasaki. Cambodia. Bosnia. Chechnya. Rwanda. Darfur. Southern Sudan. East Congo. These are more than geographical locations. They are bleak reminders that injustice and violence, despite the teachings of the world's religions, have not decreased but have intensified. If anything, the destruction of human life since the early decades of the twentieth century, including the first decade of this century, makes the biblical stories of war appear as an early form of "business as usual."

When World War II broke out in 1939, Adolf Hitler and his Nazi leaders began a massive program to "purify" the population of Europe. Their method was simple: mass murder. Their targets included all European Jews in what humanity now remembers as the *Shoah* (a Hebrew word for "catastrophe") or the Holocaust. They also began a systematic destruction of the Gypsy (Romani) peoples, the mentally ill and physically disabled, homosexuals, political dissidents, as well as the political and cultural leaders of Poland and the Soviet Union.

The Crime without a Name

As the German SS police and military personnel inflicted widespread atrocities in the wake of their early military campaigns, Winston Churchill, the British prime minister, stated in August 1941: "We are in the presence of a crime without a name." In 1944, Raphael Lemkin, a Polish-born Jew who had moved to Washington, D.C., and worked for the U.S. government, found a name for this crime against humanity. In his book *Axis Rule in Occupied Europe,* he coined the term "genocide."[3]

There is a sad irony here. It wasn't until the Second World War that Western civilization created the term "genocide" to describe the systematic extermination of entire groups of people. But such atrocities have existed in one form or another throughout history. We need only revisit the story of our nation to confirm this sobering truth. The European immigrants who came to this continent—whether by political circumstance or collective fear—engaged in forms of violence that decimated or severely diminished the population of the native peoples. This "trail of tears" reflects a grim litany of places and people: Wounded Knee, Sand Creek, Bad Axe, Bear River, Humboldt Bay, and Washita River. There are those who argue that there were atrocities on both sides, and that these were "painful accidents of history" rather than genocide as we define it today.[4] But for Native Americans whose ancestors experienced these tragedies, the technicalities of language offer little comfort. And they certainly don't change the outcome.

Many had hoped that the Second World War would bring an end to the brutality of totalitarian regimes and the madness of inflated nationalism. Unfortunately, this has not been the case. The following is a brief summary of one dimension of human violence in the last six decades. It is a tragic narrative, but it is part of our contemporary human story.

Following World War II, in 1948, the UN Convention on the Prevention and Punishment of the Crime of Genocide was unanimously adopted. The Convention entered into force on January 12, 1951, after more than twenty countries from around the world ratified it. Ironically it was not until 1988 that the United States, over the opposition of those who feared it would jeopardize national sovereignty, finally signed the UN Convention on the Prevention and Punishment of Genocide.

In the wake of World War II, crimes against civilian populations continued on a massive scale, often greeted with silence or, at best, political hand wringing in the wider international community. Not a single country appealed to the Genocide Convention when the Khmer Rouge (1975-1979) regime in Cambodia caused the deaths of an estimated 1.7 million people. Any hope that such an international agreement might prevent or even curb this outrage has been all but lost.

From 1991 to 1995 widespread crimes against humanity were committed during the series of conflicts in the former Yugoslavia. The international community was shocked to learn that in Bosnia ethnic cleansing, rape, and mass murder were an integral tactic in the "art of war." In the town of Srebrenica, for instance, nearly eight thousand men and boys were murdered by Serbian forces.[5]

The world watched in horror and apparent helplessness in 1994 when up to eight hundred thousand people, primarily from the Tutsi minority and politically moderate Hutus were killed in Rwanda. The mass murders were calculated, swift, and devastatingly widespread. What makes this story all the more shocking is that private citizens were frequently called on by local officials and government-sponsored radio stations to kill their neighbors. Those who refused to kill were often murdered themselves. Most of the victims were put to death in their villages or towns, often by their neighbors or fellow villagers. Many of the self-described "militia" murdered their victims with weapons furnished by army units or by hacking them with machetes. Victims were frequently found hiding in churches and school buildings, where Hutu gangs massacred them.[6]

As was the case in earlier forms of ethnic cleansing, the violence in Rwanda included rape as a brutal tool of genocide. The investigations that followed this tragedy uncovered evidence that military leaders encouraged—and in some cases ordered—the militia to rape Tutsi women. The amount of organized propaganda and gender-based hate literature that helped fuel sexual violence against women is staggering. So blatant was this practice that in 1998, the International Criminal Tribunal for Rwanda made a landmark decision that "war rape" in Rwanda was an essential aspect of the crime of genocide.[7]

The 2004 film *Hotel Rwanda* portrays a true story about the hotelier Paul Rusesabagina and his courageous attempts to save the lives of his family and more than a thousand other refugees by sheltering them in the besieged Hôtel des Mille Collines during the time of the genocide. It has been referred to by some critics as an "African Schindler's List" and is listed by the American Film Institute as one of the one hundred most inspirational films of all time.

Each decade brings new "killing fields" to our global consciousness. As this is being written, Darfur and East Congo are experiencing widespread suffering and death. Technically, the conflicts in Darfur and Congo have been portrayed as civil wars that began—in the case of East Congo—more than a decade ago. However, most human rights activists, as well as the U.S. government, maintain that these wars are in reality political and military excuses for outright genocide. Even by the most conservative estimates, several million people have been killed. In addition, almost 2.5 million citizens of Darfur have been forced to flee their homes and are living in refugee camps.

The majority of the deaths in Darfur resulted from malnutrition and exposure, as civilians were forcibly displaced into the harsh desert environment. A massive aid effort that began in 2003 saved countless lives and stemmed the death toll. As the conflict has continued, however, humanitarian aid workers themselves have increasingly become targets of violence.

Recent reports indicate that the atrocities, mass murders, rapes, torture, and mutilation in East Congo are more widespread and devastating than in any other country.[8] After a dozen years of conflict, it is estimated that almost six million lives have been destroyed, not to mention the untold suffering of millions of others who have—for good or for ill—survived. For the most part, the rest of the world has either ignored this violence or observed it from a distance without an effective humanitarian response.

Violence and War in the Bible

With this brief history of contemporary violence as a sobering backdrop, we turn now to our religious traditions. War and human violence are a tragic part of human history, so understandably they are also vividly described in the collection of writings that we hold as sacred. War is so common in the Hebrew Scriptures that times of peace are specifically mentioned (Judg 3:11; 1 Kgs 5:4; 2 Chr 14:5-7), perhaps because they were unusual and even surprising.

The Bible isn't just a book; it is an entire library that came into being over the course of millennia, spanning many lifetimes and historical eras. It began as oral stories and teachings that were eventually collected, edited, and finally written down. Thus, in the Hebrew and Christian Scriptures we encounter a wide diversity of literary forms, including creation stories, ritual laws, historical accounts, psalms, wisdom sayings, priestly tracts, and prophetic utterances. In the pages of the Bible, we also confront an evolution of ethics and a diversity of religious convictions. Not surprisingly, people have read the Bible from the perspective of their ethical worldview and for their own purposes. Over the centuries, the Scriptures have been quoted to defend actions and institutions that are now universally understood to be immoral. For example, the Bible was frequently cited as a justification for slavery and the oppression of women. It is still used today to rationalize unjust wars, capital punishment, and discrimination toward sexual minorities.

How can we make sense of this? To begin with, it is important to acknowledge that we are reflecting on an extensive journey of human consciousness. Our sacred writings reflect a prolonged ethical evolution in which we have come to revise and reimage concepts such as protection, solidarity, covenant, community, justice, and even the meaning of the term "God." To state the obvious, we are still engaged in this shared learning curve today.

The most responsible way to approach the Bible is by recognizing that our understanding of God has evolved over the centuries. Most biblical scholars, along with serious believers, have long acknowledged this fact. Since our language and images of God are inherently dependent on our human experience, our description of God will change along with the evolution of our self-understanding. Over the last two decades several books have traced this evolution and its consequences.[9] "The human idea of God," writes Karen Armstrong, "has a history, since it has always meant something slightly different to each group of people who have used it at various points of time."[10]

Recent surveys confirm that the majority of people in the United States believe in God. The question is *which* God? Are we speaking of the god of mythic consciousness? Or the god of the clans and tribes who survived by blood vengeance and the threat of extermination? Are we referring to the god of the early nation-states with their goal of military victory at any cost? In the Scriptures there are portraits of God ranging from creator to destroyer, from liberator to lawgiver, from protector of the poor to perpetrator of vengeance, from executioner to the transcendent Holy One, from friend to fiend.[11]

Some of the scriptural descriptions of God are mysterious and puzzling; others are shocking and dreadful. In the story of Abraham and Sarah, an elderly childless couple is finally promised a child, only to learn that the same God is now commanding Abraham to take his son, Isaac, to Mount Moriah and offer him as a sacrifice. In the central narrative of the exodus, God leads the people to freedom. But by what means? First, he (clearly a male version of the divine) sends ten fearful plagues upon the people of Egypt. He turns the Nile to blood, ravages the land with locusts and frogs, and plunges the countryside into impenetrable darkness. But the most savage punishment is saved for last: he sends the Angel of Death to kill the firstborn sons of all the Egyptians.[12]

However scholars might explain this in terms of anthropomorphic language or cultural practices that have been projected onto the deity, the god that is portrayed here is, to put it bluntly, vicious and vengeful. This is the god that came to be known as *Yahweh Sabaoth*—which in Hebrew means "the Lord of the armies"—the warrior God. This is the god who commands Joshua to destroy the Canaanite cities. Thirty-one towns are destroyed and all their inhabitants killed, including women and children. Only the cattle and other spoils of war are spared (Josh 8:26-27). In today's terms, this can only be characterized as a narrative of genocide.

Moving from Fear to Solidarity

The Book of Joshua and other similar writings reflect a primitive understanding of the deity—or more correctly, *deities*—and their imagined, projected role of advocacy on behalf of distinctive ethnic groups against their enemies. Authentic faith calls us to move beyond these versions of religious entitlement and overzealous forms of nationalism. The "Lord of armies" is not the God of the later prophets or the emerging vision of biblical justice. It is not the God of Jesus. Nor is it the core human ethic that we have claimed for our emerging global community. The United Nations' condemnation of genocide, along with its Charter on Human Rights is, at the very least, a mandate that integrates the deepest ethical values of the world religions.

The challenge facing us is immense. In today's polarized world, there are religious believers who claim a version of God that ultimately justifies hatred, terrorism, ethnic violence, and unjust wars. This stance of self-righteousness creates an ongoing atmosphere of fear and suspicion. It explains why neither genocide nor war erupts spontaneously. On the contrary, they are the outcome of years, even centuries, of suspicion and resentment toward the "other." This simmering hatred is in turn fueled by irresponsible, power-hungry political leaders who manipulate these ancient resentments through propaganda. Tragically, religious fanaticism often heightens these tensions, and the resulting social hysteria eventually erupts into violence. The cycle of mass murder repeats itself.

The first step toward ending this cycle involves a radical reform of religion itself. Our spiritual traditions are challenged to shift from a focus on rigid orthodoxy toward a commitment to "orthopraxy"—a concern to unite people in the spirit of solidarity instead of fracturing them with further claims to doctrinal purity. Truth matters, but the deepest form of truth is the practice of compassion. This will require our traditions to shift their focus from belief systems that define people over and against others, and instead to acknowledge the earth as our common heritage and to celebrate the shared humanity that unites us.

RESPECTING THE OTHER

The second step is more personal but no less demanding. It challenges each of us to examine our conscious or subconscious fears of those who are different from us. The theologian David Tracy states that the greatest ethical challenge of the twenty-first century is to learn to respect "the other." This has little to do with sentimentalism or being politically correct. Rather, it involves the hard work of facing our fears and naming our demons, of being honest about the reality of prejudice and subconscious forms of discrimination in our lives.

In the late 1950s I left my roots in rural Wisconsin to pursue university studies in Washington, D.C. Until then I had never traveled beyond the Midwest. I lived in a part of the country that, at that time, was primarily white Euro-American in its ethnic makeup. Even so, I considered myself to be an open, tolerant person who had few if any prejudices. The day after I arrived in Washington, I took public transportation to visit the national monuments. As I was getting on the bus and finding a seat, I recognized that I was—for the first time in my awareness—in the minority. Most of my fellow passengers were African Americans. Nothing surprising here, since I already knew that the majority of the D.C. residents were black. What was disturbing was not my observation but the emotions that it stirred in me. I was afraid. Where was this uneasiness coming from? I held strong convictions about the equality of races and the dignity of every human person. Then why was I fearful?

Looking back on that experience I realize that I can respond to this question in several different ways. But most of my answers, to be honest, are not particularly helpful. Perhaps I was uncomfortable because I was outside my familiar surroundings. Maybe I was uneasy because this was beyond my psychic comfort zone or because I was suddenly thrust into a socially unknown environment. True enough. But the deeper truth is this: whatever my personal convictions, my white cultural background had created a subconscious fear of African American people. I may not have been consciously prejudiced, but the churning in my stomach told me that I had inherited an ancient suspicion of the "other." It was, to put it mildly, an instructive moment in my process of maturing.

What does respecting the other look like in practice? It involves both a change in attitude and a transformation of behaviors. First comes the change in attitude; and in many ways this is the most demanding shift of all. Change is inevitable, but this kind of intentional conversion of attitude is clearly optional and difficult. It is the challenge that the poet W. H. Auden describes:

> We would rather be ruined than changed.
> We would rather die in our dread
> Than climb the cross of the moment
> And let our illusions die.[13]

The cross of the moment for the human community—and for each of us—is to shift our perspective from competition to cooperation, from suspicion to respect, from fear to openness. Obviously, this is a call to conversion on both a personal and a communal level, a summons to change for individuals, institutions, and cultural structures.

WIDENING THE CIRCLE

Respecting the other implies a willingness to draw our relational maps on a larger scale. "Enlarge the site of your tent," Isaiah tells the exiles, "and let the curtains of your habitations be stretched out" (Isa 54:2). In this case, the prophet was still speaking from a more exclusivist perspective, but his admonition is timely for the tasks that we face today. Each of us is invited to "enlarge the site our tents"—our ways of thinking, our manner of approaching other people. Our religious institutions are similarly challenged to "stretch out" their perspectives to include other points of view, different paths to truth, distinct ways of loving and being loved.

This is no small task. In the history of humanity, competition and exclusion have tended to be the primary focus, not cooperation or inclusion. Each ethnic and spiritually distinct group appears to have the habit of locating the *axis mundi*, the center of the world, within its territorial boundaries, both geographically and religiously. Jerusalem, Rome, and Mecca are more than physical locations. They are internalized metaphors of spiritual and cultural worlds.

In his book *Black Elk Speaks*, the poet John Neihardt describes a scene in which an old Sioux medicine man, the Keeper of the Sacred Pipe for his people, recalls the formative vision of his youth. In his prophetic imagination he saw himself standing on the central mountain of the world:

> I was seeing in a sacred manner the shapes of all things in the spirit, and the shape of all things as they must live together, like one being. And I saw that the sacred hoop of my people was one of many hoops that made one circle, wide as daylight and as starlight, and in the center grew one mighty flowering tree to shelter all the children of one mother and one father.[14]

The central mountain in this scene is not Jerusalem, Rome, or Mecca. It is in the Black Hills of South Dakota. When the human spirit "enlarges its tent" the *axis mundi* expands and becomes more inclusive. Or, as Black Elk puts it, "anywhere is the center of the world."[15]

Black Elk's vision echoes the wisdom of an early medieval text: "God is an infinite sphere, whose center is everywhere and whose circumference is nowhere."[16] To state it in more earthy language: Every bush is on fire. Every field is sacred ground. Every lake carries the bath of life. Every path is pilgrimage. Every sea is the mother water; and every human being is an image of the holy. This shift in human consciousness is quietly emerging in today's world. It is appearing not on banner headlines, in political policy, or in military strategy, but in the common intuition of grassroots believers. Accompanying this intuition is a realistic awareness: this will not be easy. Peace, unlike war, will not "break out." Despite our popular assumptions, peace-making is a far more demanding, disciplined task than preparing for or fighting a war. And, before it is an action, making peace is first a transformed stance of the heart.

All Real Living Is Meeting

The Jewish philosopher and mystic Martin Buber died on June 13, 1965, after a lifetime dedicated to promoting a spirit of dialogue, respect, and understanding among people. At his funeral in Jerusalem an unprecedented event took place. The predominantly Jewish congregation was stunned to see a delegation of Arab students come slowly forward to lay a wreath near Buber's remains. In the face of bitter animosity between the Arab and Israeli people, Buber's vision of dialogue had come true—if only for a moment—at the time of his death. On his coffin there was inscribed the simple motto by which he lived his life: "All real living is meeting."

Martin Buber spent his life promoting human mutuality and respect. In his masterful book *I and Thou*, Buber speaks of the difference between I–Thou and I–It relationships.[17] When one person—as a center of reflective consciousness—addresses another as a "Thou" it is with the awareness that we are ultimately united and share the gift of life. On the other hand, when a human ego addresses another person as an "It" the result is to separate oneself over and against the other, reducing that person to an object or a member of an "out-group," and thereby a potential enemy. The central challenge today is to surrender our exclusivity, to set aside those distinctions that define us over and against one another. This is not primarily a political issue. It is before all else a spiritual and religious challenge. If our spiritual traditions can reclaim their primal vision and purpose, they will begin to create a renewed path toward justice and peace.

3

Confronting Violence

Refocusing Our Religious Priorities

*While you are proclaiming peace with your lips, be careful to
have it even more fully in your heart.*
> —Francis of Assisi

*Beneath the problem of empire is the problem of justice, but
beneath the problem of justice is the problem of violence.*
> —John Dominic Crossan

In the late 1960s I attended a conference on international development and its relation to justice and peace. The meeting was held in
New York City only a few blocks from the United Nations, so one evening I took a slow, reflective walk through the complex and its surrounding gardens. Close to the General Assembly Building, on the
banks of the East River, there is the famous bronze statue by the
Russian artist Yevgeny Vuchetich, *Let Us Beat Swords into Plowshares*.
Across the street in a small park, carved into a wall, are the words of
Isaiah that the statue strives to embody:

> They shall beat their swords into plowshares,
> and their spears into pruning hooks;
> nation shall not lift up sword against nation,
> neither shall they learn war any more. (Isa 2:4)

As the sun set behind me and the city's skyscrapers, I lingered
in front of the statue. Two questions circled quietly in the back of
my mind. The first was, Is this merely a sentimental wish, or is it

a genuine call to conversion? The second was, Is Isaiah describing a dream for the distant future, or is he addressing the critical now of every historical era? As is clear from these reflections, I believed then—and continue to hold as a conviction now—that the answer is found in the second half of each question. Isaiah was not offering pious sentiments. He was demanding a change of heart. He was not speaking of someday. He was mandating a transformation of attitude and action for today as it shapes the hope of all our tomorrows.

THE PROPHETIC TASK

In his still timely book *The Prophetic Imagination*, Walter Brueggemann confronts the false assumptions that we bring to prophecy, as well as naming the authentic role that prophets have in every generation. One of the usual misperceptions is that prophets are future-tellers. While the language of prophecy often refers to impending events, the prophet's primary concern is the present, not the future. Brueggemann describes the mission of the prophet in these terms:

> *The task of prophetic ministry is to nurture, nourish, and evoke a consciousness and perception alternative to the consciousness and perception of the dominant culture around us. Thus I sug-*gest that prophetic ministry has to do not primarily with addressing specific public crises but with addressing in season and out of season, the dominant crisis that is enduring and resilient, of having our alternative vocation co-opted and domesticated.[1]

To state this in a different way, religious institutions require a prophetic dimension to prevent them from becoming "tamed" by political structures that are oppressive, violent, or unjust. Most religious traditions have three integral components:

- a *creed* that articulates a fundamental spiritual vision;
- a *code* of moral conduct that tells its adherents how to live out that vision in their daily lives;
- a *cult*, or a set of ritual practices that celebrates the adherents' vision and practice in communal worship.

These three dimensions of religion—creed, code, and cult—are necessary and helpful aspects of any faith tradition. Given the human condition, however, there is a built-in drift, a gradual slide toward being co-opted by the dominant culture in such a way that religion simply becomes a convenient tool to conduct business as usual for the ruling class. In short, creed drifts toward dogmatism; morality easily slips into legalism; and worship frequently falls into ritualism.

The prophet has the ongoing task of reclaiming the original spiritual vision and shaping it for a new time. This task has two creative dimensions, each of which unfolds in tension with the other. The first prophetic task is to *criticize* the dominant culture in those aspects that are blunting the human spirit, oppressing the dignity of individuals, or fragmenting the moral fiber of a community. The second is to *energize* the people by calling them to deeper conversion and by offering the promise of renewal through self-sacrifice and solidarity with those who suffer injustice.[2]

It is not easy to hold these two responsibilities in a creative balance. Either we become so preoccupied with criticism and resentment that we trade one form of oppression for another, or we are so intent on energizing the community that we fail to risk speaking the truth to structures of power. Given this challenge, when prophets manage to criticize *and* energize, it is not surprising that most of them are not welcomed, let alone taken seriously. It also explains why most of them face rejection and a life of suffering.

These chapters focus on the task of creating justice and peace in our Judeo-Christian tradition, but we cannot understand our tradition without placing it in the wider context of the prophets and sages in other spiritual traditions. Human beings are inherently religious. From the earliest artifacts, cave paintings, and other primal images, there is evidence that we are meaning-seeking creatures. The hunger for God is like a pilot light in the core of our psyche. It burns as a quiet, persistent flame to remind us of the eternal longing in our hearts. From our first cry as infants until we draw our last breath, something in us reaches for transcendence. Whether we ever find the words for it or not, we seek to know the source of our being and the destiny that awaits us, the mystery that sustains and encompasses our every breath. Jesus captures this communal sense of pilgrimage: "I came from the Father and have come into the world; again, I am leaving the world and am going to the Father" (John 16:28). Life is a journey, and time is the river. We enter this stream from an eternal source, and, like all those who have gone before us, it carries us toward a destiny beyond our comprehension.

Many scholars believe that the etymological origin of religion (*religio*, to bind together again) is related to reconnecting with the source of life and existence. One might assume, then, that religion would be primarily about creating the conditions that foster bonds of communion between human beings and the larger web of life. At its best, religion has served this vision well. But it is not always at its best. When authentic spiritual commitment is operative, it focuses on compassion as the highest form of ethical behavior. But when religion loses its primary purpose or is co-opted by political and cultural forces, it can easily become fanatical, even cruel in its pursuit of compliance and truth.

COMPASSION IN THE FACE OF VIOLENCE: THE FIRST AXIAL AGE

In her writings, Karen Armstrong has helped us understand both the power and the ambivalence of religion and its relation to violence. In her masterful study *The Great Transformation,* she explores the emergence of the world religions as they confront the rise of injustice and aggression in the human community.[3] There are two pivotal periods in human history that give us insight into the role of religion and violence, spirituality and peacemaking. The first unfolded almost three thousand years ago; the second is emerging quietly in our contemporary world.

In the 1940s the German existentialist philosopher Karl Jaspers coined the term "axial period" to refer to the enormous flowering of culture, religion, and rational thought that emerged from about 900 to 200 BCE. He referred to it as an "axial" era because it proved to be a pivotal time in human history. During these centuries human consciousness was teeming with new visions and discoveries. During this period the major world religions emerged, including Confucianism and Daoism in China, Hinduism and Buddhism in India, monotheism in Israel, and rational philosophy in Greece. Christianity, Rabbinic Judaism, and Islam are the later flowering of this time of intense spiritual stirring.

According to Armstrong, this spiritual renewal came about as a response to the growing fierceness of violence and war. Early in this period humans had discovered how to manufacture tools made from iron. This breakthrough not only improved agriculture and other aspects of civilization; it also created more lethal weapons for war. Thus, the cultures that we now refer to as the "cradles of civilization" became increasingly aggressive and warlike. Although their weapons appear primitive compared to today's nuclear arsenals and high-tech warfare, the outcome was widespread conflict, oppression, and brutality.

These new tools of human technology literally revolutionized the landscape of social interaction. Sweeping changes took place in the forms of agricultural production and the exchange of goods. The early cities came into being, with their concentration of population and new models of commerce. It was no longer just the kings and priests who exercised social and religious control. Political and economic power was also shifting to the marketplace. Those who benefited least from these developments were, of course, the lower classes and the poor. For them it meant only new and more painful encounters with inequality and exploitation.

These economic and political developments in turn triggered growth in other areas of the human psyche. The conflict and crises of this age occasioned a deepening of reflection, an inwardness that became the birthing place of a powerful spiritual renewal. Women and men were confronted with daily reminders of their mortality. They began to ask new and more urgent questions about the meaning of existence and the search for authentic happiness. Several of the sacred stories that emerged during this time reflect the loss of a past "primeval" time, as well as the need to come to grips with the limits of the human condition, especially the haunting specter of death. The Neolithic revolution—the gradual shift from hunting and gathering to the complexities of agricultural and urban life—is the larger context for this growth in interiority as well as the deeper encounter with human insecurity.

Two brief examples can illustrate the ways in which the human spirit was trying to understand and respond to the Neolithic revolution. The first is the Sumerian myth of Gilgamesh; the second is what is known as the Yahwist version of creation (Genesis 2-3).

GILGAMESH AND THE QUEST FOR IMMORTALITY

The Epic of Gilgamesh is probably the oldest written story in human history. It comes to us from ancient Sumeria and recounts the adventures of the historical king of Uruk (about 2750-2500 BCE). Behind the twelve panels of cuneiform writing that were recovered early in the twentieth century are not one, but more likely five epics that were handed on orally for centuries and finally collected together in written form. As complex and nuanced as this epic is, it is far more than an adventure story. It is an early meditation on the fundamental questions of emerging human consciousness: the use of violence in the pursuit of fame, the tasks of responsibility, the value of friendship, the experience of loss, and, most of all, the inevitability and mystery of death, with its parallel longing for eternal life.

The story of Gilgamesh reflects the transition of human consciousness from the tribal-warrior-hero to the king of a walled city-state that would have been characteristic of the evolving civilization at that time. He is the mythic strongman whose unrestrained ego and drive toward power make him more of a tyrant than a servant of the people. His inner struggle to discover his humanity is mirrored in his outer combat with Enkidu, a wild man who signifies the natural, earlier "uncivilized" world of what today we call the Paleolithic era. Eventually the two become friends and set out on adventures together. When Enkidu dies, Gilgamesh is devastated and, in his grief, sets out to find his friend in the underworld. He is also seeking the key to personal immortality. In the process he must cross the river of Death to find Utnapishtim, who has achieved immortality by surviving the great flood (an early source of the story of Noah, Genesis 6-9).

Gilgamesh is the archetype of the later literary figures that embody the theme of *quest*, ranging from Odysseus, Aeneas, Parsifal, and Faust to contemporary accounts of the human spirit seeking life and meaning. Like many of these figures, Gilgamesh eventually finds his way home. He returns to Uruk, not with the secret of immortality but with the sober realization that he must embrace finitude and death as part of the human condition.

GENESIS 2-3: BECOMING HUMAN

In the Yahwist account of creation, we have a different version of humankind's journey toward reflective consciousness. The earth creature (*ha 'adam*) is formed out of the dust of the earth and brought to life as God breathes into its clay. Through a mysterious transformation (described in the poetic language of a "deep sleep"), the earth creature evolves into *'ish* (the man, Adam) and *'ishah* (the woman, who is eventually named Eve, the mother of the living). Next, comes the familiar story of the two trees in the middle of the garden—the tree of life and the tree of the knowledge of good and evil. Metaphorically, the first tree represents eternal life or immortality; the second tree represents moral knowledge, or the emergence of reflective self-awareness and human freedom with their profound consequences.

In his insightful commentary on this Genesis story, John Dominic Crossan gives us a helpful perspective on the dawning challenge that the primal couple faced: "Divinity had the attributes of both trees, but humanity could only have one or the other. Humans could have eternal life *or* moral knowledge, but not eternal life *and* moral knowledge. That was for God alone."[4]

God therefore tells the first humans: "You may freely eat of every tree of the garden; but of the tree of the knowledge of good and evil you shall not eat, for in the day that you eat of it you shall die" (2:16-17). In the ensuing temptation scene, however, the serpent says to the woman: "You will not die; for God knows that when you eat of it your eyes will be opened, and you will be like God, knowing good and evil" (3:4-5).

How are we to interpret this? First, we should notice that the tempter is a *serpent*. In the ancient world of hunting and gathering, of sacred seasons and the goddess, the serpent—in its capacity to shed its skin and be "reborn"—was revered as an image of the resilience of life and its rhythmic return. It is no accident that the serpent is both literally and metaphorically "demonized" in this story. The ancient oral traditions from which this story originated reflect the antagonism of the emerging transcendent male divinity, Yahweh, toward the earlier goddess-based religions that were still practiced by Israel's neighbors.

Second, the serpent is actually telling the truth, though only partially. The primal couple does not die, at least not when they eat of the tree of the knowledge of good and evil. On the other hand, they become aware that they, like all the rest of living creatures, will indeed die someday.[5] Their sudden realization of being "naked" is a poetic way of saying that they are conscious of their mortality, their finitude. They are also "naked" before the mystery of freedom. As self-conscious creatures who have the gift of free choice and intentionality, they have indeed become like God in one vital respect: they know good and evil, because they must now choose between them.

Theologians would later interpret this story as the "fall" or the "original sin" of disobedience toward God. Many contemporary writers, however, understand this scene in a different light.[6] They see it not as a fall downward into sin but as the dawn of moral consciousness. Human beings are leaving the world of instinct, the pre-conscious state of "innocence" and entering the world of responsibility. Hence, it is not sin itself that is described here, but the condition of the possibility of *choosing* sin—of embracing selfishness and violence in the pursuit of privilege and power. Eating of the tree of the knowledge of good and evil is a metaphorical way of describing an awakening from a pre-conscious state into becoming a self-conscious ego. Nakedness is not about clothes but about the dawning awareness of being a separate, unfinished pilgrim on this earth. Similarly, the expulsion from paradise is a poetic way of describing the loneliness of the human condition—our sense of no longer experiencing oneness with God, creation, or with our sisters and brothers. It is, in brief, a metaphor for humanity beginning to grow up, to leave nature and to begin creating culture.

It is likewise an introduction to the world of violence, oppression, and injustice. All human beings—including each of us—have, in fact, chosen to sin. In our secular culture, this is no longer a politically correct way of describing our human failings. But softening the language does not change the wreckage of human history. "Sin" is simply another way of saying that, at crucial times in our lives, we have "missed the point" of what it means to be fellow pilgrims. The rest of the story in Genesis is what happens when human beings lose this deeper purpose of life and instead pursue their own agenda at the expense of their sisters and brothers. From that point forward, they face the dangerous tasks of developing civilization. Specifically, they must now confront their loneliness and finitude. They must carry the burden of freedom and live with responsibility. In the ancient mythic archetype, Prometheus has stolen the fire from the gods. For good or for ill, the flame of consciousness and choice is now burning in the human psyche.

Creation and our participation in it are a gift, but also a responsibility. In its long journey toward maturity, humankind has struggled with both of these mysteries. We have often neglected the gift, and we have frequently misused our responsibility. From as early as we can remember, we began to choose power over partnership, competition over cooperation. Civilization both mirrors and creates the spiraling violence between individuals and nations. Civilization begins in fratricide. Cain, the farmer, kills Abel, the shepherd. Farming becomes the resource for building cities, reflected in the story of the tower of Babel, and, along with it, the further escalation of violence.

The stories of Gilgamesh and Genesis reflect two differing perspectives on how humanity emerged and the challenges that it faces in relation to God and creation. Whatever the differences, there are some underlying common themes that are worth noting:

- Both stories understand human beings as emerging from and *rooted in creation*—in the natural world. They do not use our more scientific or theological language of evolution, but clearly they see humanity as formed from the earth and its energies.
- The awakening of what today we describe as *moral consciousness* or responsibility is outlined in poetic imagery in both stories. We see the ambivalence that flows from freedom—the capacity, indeed the burden, of choosing between good and evil, between reverence and exploitation.
- Both accounts deal with the *sense of loss and alienation* (leaving nature, leaving the garden) that arises from what we today refer to as the Neolithic revolution—the slow shift from hunting and gathering to the emerging civilization based on stable agriculture and the emerging city-state.
- Gilgamesh and Genesis both address the central question of human finitude and the *mystery of death* as part of the pilgrimage of human existence.
- When we become aware of our mortality, we also struggle with anxiety and insecurity. These stories point to the usual *psychic responses to this insecurity*: hiding, blaming, conflict, alienation, and eventually the acquisition of weapons and the struggle for resources.
- Finally, both of these stories attempt to portray the brokenness of human existence by describing the *escalation of violence* and the expanding phenomenon of injustice. Their images and metaphors capture the painful fault line of violence that lies beneath the surface of the human community.

WISDOM FOR LIVING

How did people of the first axial age respond to the endless wars that engulfed their lives and consumed their resources? The more reflective members of these societies saw the need to renew their religious structures, many of which had drifted into shallow rituals, or worse yet, had been sabotaged by the ruling powers to promote their political goals.

But their concern went beyond renewing the traditional ceremonies. They saw the need to shape an entirely new spiritual vision and practice, a way of life that transcended the systems controlled by the kings and priests. As institutions failed to respond to the crisis, these reflective individuals looked for new horizons and broke away from the older traditions. They were convinced that a different way of viewing spiritual values and ethical behavior needed to emerge. Instead of looking for change in external structures, they began to explore the depth of their inner selves, seeking a new inwardness and striving to honor others by becoming one with transcendent reality.

In their journey inward, these spiritual pilgrims unearthed the foundational values of what we know today as the perennial philosophy: that existence is wider and deeper than what we can see; that there is a transcendent reality at the heart of life. They also named the core values that the major world religions have in common, namely, a shared ethic regarding the preciousness of life, the dignity of the human person, and a stance of radical respect. Most of all they discovered a new way of being conscious, a deeper manner of finding life through compassion.[7] ← CMM

In almost every instance, the spiritualities of the axial age arose out of a concern regarding violence. They mirror the human spirit struggling with itself, wrestling with brutality and seeking to find a different way of creating harmony with other people. Whether we are speaking of Confucius and Lao Tzu in China; Siddhartha and the monks of the Indian Subcontinent; the tragedian playwrights, Socrates, and Plato in ancient Greece; or Isaiah, Micah, Amos, and the other prophets of Israel, all of them speak of compassion as the foundational ethic for all religion, and justice as the way in which compassion is most visibly enfleshed.

This essential vision of compassion is summed up in the golden rule, which was first enunciated by Confucius around 500 BCE: "Do not do unto others as you would not have them do unto you." In the first axial age, therefore, violence and human suffering functioned as the crucible for a quantum spiritual leap. Religion as a movement of the spirit became more and more identified with a life of compassion, a commitment to justice, and the power of nonviolence to transform individuals and perhaps even the institutional structures of society.

THE SECOND AXIAL AGE:
RECLAIMING COMPASSION AND JUSTICE

According to Armstrong and other scholars of religion, we are currently in the midst of a second axial age, a time in our history in which humanity faces many of the same crises, but now with greater urgency. The roots of our contemporary transition lie in the sixteenth and seventeenth centuries with the Enlightenment and the scientific revolution. Since that time Western civilization has continued to function as the engine of technological and social transformation. A myriad of forces—political, intellectual, religious, cultural, economic—have contributed to the shaping of this new world. Its primary tool is a scientific, rational approach to truth.

We have received abundant gifts from this way of reasoning. In the areas of our world where these benefits can be reaped, new medical breakthroughs have taken place; infant deaths are decreasing; the standard of living has increased; people are living longer. But despite our technological breakthroughs and our scientific discoveries, these advances have not lowered the level of violence in the world. If anything, they have increased its intensity and the scale of devastation.

Even as we name this sobering reality, it is essential to acknowledge another truth. Science is a tool, an instrument of our invention; it is not the cause of violence. Only we human beings can claim that responsibility. Thus, it is even more tragic that our faith traditions have not been able to challenge this rising tide of bloodshed. Our faith has its roots in the first axial period, but despite the soaring rhetoric of our traditions, religion has been largely impotent to stop the escalation of violence. In many instances, religion—in its more dogmatic and fundamentalist expressions—has actually functioned as an instrument of repression and a rationale for terrorism or war.

The scientific rationalists of the nineteenth and twentieth centuries anticipated that humankind would outgrow religion as though it were a childlike need of earlier generations. Today we are witnessing a new wave of atheism that provides an updated version of the former arguments. These "new atheists" are articulate, harsh, and unrelenting in their critique of religion. Their books dismiss anyone who believes in the transcendent as deluded or intellectually immature. Despite their hostile appraisals and those of their predecessors, religion is thriving. However, this is not the same as saying that religion is alive and well. Atheism is often more of a protest than a policy, a confrontation of shallow and misdirected religion rather than a full-blown alternative to faith. In other words, the atheists' critique, however virulent or unfair, deserves to be taken seriously.

The question is not whether or not we should be religious. The question is what *focus* our religious practice ought to have. If we continue to concentrate on being dogmatically correct, how will this change people's lives? How will it enable us to confront systems of oppression? This is not to say that orthodoxy is unimportant; it is only to emphasize that correct doctrine in itself will not transform attitudes or behavior. The challenge we are facing today is not unlike that of the monks and prophets of the first axial age. Armstrong states it in these terms:

> What mattered was not what you believed but how you behaved. Religion was about doing things that changed you at a profound level. Before the Axial Age, ritual and animal sacrifice had been central to the religious quest. You experienced the divine in sacred dramas that, like a great theatrical experience today, introduced you to another level of existence. The Axial sages changed this; they still valued ritual, but gave it a new ethical significance and put morality at the heart of the spiritual life. The only way you could encounter what they called "God," "Nirvana," "Brahman," or the "Way" was to live a compassionate life. Indeed, religion was compassion.[8]

The Roman Catholic teachings on compassion and social justice are strong and decisive. The difficulty is that they are not often given the prominence or priority that the conditions of our age demand. The Second Vatican Council reiterated the central vision of the gospel: "The joys and hopes, the grief and anguish of the people of our time, especially of those who are poor and afflicted, are the joys and hopes, the grief and anguish of the followers of Christ as well" (*Gaudium et Spes* #1).[9] These words speak of the urgency of nurturing and protecting human life—and indeed all created life—from womb to tomb. They could serve as an apt mission statement for our contemporary communities of faith.

The escalating violence in our world is summoning us to a new spiritual revolution. Our crises are similar and yet different from the first axial age. Compared to that time, our conflicts have become, in Christopher Fry's poetic image, "soul size." But these ancient wisdom

figures are still a source of insight for our lives. In the face of our growing potential for self-destruction, there is an essential wisdom that we
can learn from these spiritual sages. Like us, they were shocked by the
fear, oppression, and despair that surrounded them. They were forced
to look beyond institutions into their own hearts to discover the pat-
terns of cruelty and injustice. They discovered that greed, selfishness,
and competition made people less than their authentic selves. They
taught their followers to follow the path of compassion, to cultivate
an attitude of empathy for all creation.

In the language of the gospel, this is precisely what it means to
be a "disciple"—that we spend our lives as "apprentices" in learning
the way of selfless loving. The test of the cross is not guilt but generous service toward our sisters and brothers in the human community. Spiritual practice is not a self-focused form of escape. It is not
designed to be one more commodity to make us feel good about ourselves. A spirituality of compassion is a demanding and, at times, a
terrifying path to walk.

4

Challenging Systems of Injustice

The Hidden Violence of Civilization

They make slaughter and they call it peace.
> —Tacitus

I feed the poor, I'm called a saint. I ask why the poor have no food, I'm called a communist.
> —Dom Helder Camara

In the nineteenth century, the central moral challenge was slavery. In the twentieth century, it was the battle against totalitarianism. We believe that in this century the paramount moral challenge will be the struggle for gender equality in the developing world.
> —Nicholas Kristof and Sheryl WuDunn

Several years ago I attended a presentation by the archbishop of Recife and Olinda, Brazil—Dom Helder Camara. From the moment he walked to the podium, I realized that I was in the presence of a prophet. In appearance, he was a slight, frail-looking man, but his presence radiated strength, courage, and hope. He spoke of his commitment to live a life of prayer combined with a passionate advocacy for the poor. He described the impoverished people whom he served with love, as well as the crucial work of the *comunidades eclesiales de base*—the small faith and action communities that blossomed in the wake of liberation theology throughout much of Latin America.

I still have the notes that I took that evening. The most striking part of his message was his confrontation with *structural injustice*.

From his personal experience he knew that violence exists not just in individuals, but even more forcefully in social and political systems. Not surprisingly, this humble, fierce servant of justice was a threat to the military dictatorships of Brazil. Under the pretext of national security, Dom Helder was subjected to endless interrogations and threats to his life. His response was always the same. He told his interrogators that he was not a communist, not a Marxist; he was simply a man of the gospel who wanted to serve the poor.

That evening, standing on the stage of a university auditorium, Dom Helder reiterated the phrase for which he is best remembered: "I feed the poor, I'm called a saint. I ask why the poor have no food, I'm called a communist."

Dom Helder died on August 27, 1999, at the age of ninety. His stature and his legacy, however, have continued to grow. In the documents of the Second Vatican Council and the papal writings that followed, the church identified the reality of systemic violence and structural injustice. But few—with the obvious exception of Archbishop Oscar Romero in El Salvador—have challenged this reality with the courage of Dom Helder Camara. He continues to be a reminder that injustice runs deep and that cruelty often has a politically correct face. He challenges us to look beyond symptoms to sources, beyond the legitimate structures of government to a form of violence that is enshrined by law, sustained by the rich, protected by the powerful, and often blessed by religion.

CIVILIZATION AND EMPIRE: SYSTEMIC FORMS OF VIOLENCE

Archbishop Camara was telling the truth. He was not a communist or a Marxist. But he was a "subversive" on behalf of the gospel. He would not permit the gospel to be reduced to a private devotion or a spirituality of convenience. He refused to allow Jesus to become domesticated by religious leaders who supported an overzealous nationalism at the expense of the poor. He challenged the systemic reality of injustice and revealed the ways in which political and religious structures create what he identified as "the spiral of violence."[1]

In reflecting on the first axial age, we explored the ways in which the spiritual leaders and their followers were transformed by their lives of compassion. Their way of life bears witness to an alternate way of being that is respectful, just, and nonviolent. But as much as these monks and sages are remembered with admiration, history tells us that they were an exception, not a mainstream movement. They were not able to reshape the rising tide of violence or the political structures that sustained them.

The axial thinkers responded to the escalating hostility of their times by confronting its roots, namely, the human soul or psyche. They endeavored to change culture by transforming the individual. They challenged the violence of regimes by calling for personal conversion and resistance through a life of integrity. This is a critical effort in every age. It continues to be an ongoing need in our emerging global cultures today. But, sadly, their efforts—however courageous and visionary—have not significantly diminished the injustice in our social and political systems. The key word here is *systems*. They understood the human soul, but they were not yet aware of the power of political structures and the philosophical mind-set that maintains them.

The wisdom figures of that time did not directly address many of the crucial issues that we face today: classism, racism, sexism, or war as an instrument of national policy. In fact, they appear to have taken social structures for granted. Women and children were second-class citizens; patriarchy was a given; class distinctions maintained the status of the rich over the poor—all these realities were assumed to be part of an eternal plan. The monks and sages challenged the individual soul, but except for the striking case of the Hebrew prophets, they did not address the deeper sources of violence in the structures of civilization.

Yet it is important to add another observation. It is unrealistic to evaluate the first axial period from our historical perspective. Looking back from the vantage point of millennia, and carrying the cultural developments of centuries in our collective psyches, we can ask questions that reach beyond individual lifestyles to the cultural and political structures that foster violence in the human heart. In short, we can ask about civilization itself. What does it mean to be civilized? How integral to civilization are oppression, domination, social control, and war as instruments of political prowess?

When most of us hear the term "civilization" we think in positive terms. We assume that it refers to those qualities of a society that are praiseworthy and beneficial to the common good: art, music, dance, drama, religion, literature, and the great epics that give expression to our origins and founding vision. In this context, civilization describes the flowering of human consciousness through the rule of law.

Approximately ten thousand years ago, humankind began the transition from hunting and gathering to agriculture, including the domestication of animals, irrigation, and development of grains and other stable crops. The practice of agriculture, in turn, brought about the growth of an urban population, since some citizens were now free to engage in other human pursuits. Thus, during this era we witness the emergence of writing, literacy, law, metallurgy, and commerce. These in turn necessitated a ruling class, a military establishment, a priestly caste, and increasingly complex, centralized forms of government. The three most visible symbols of civilization were written records, walled cities, and sacred temples. Or to put it another way, writing for commerce, walls for military protection, and temples to ritualize and sustain civic identity.[2] While all of these developments brought immense benefits, they also came with human costs, including disease, the abuse of power, constant wars, and the increasing gap between the rich and the poor, the powerful and the vulnerable.

Civilization is likely an inevitable outcome of social and political evolution. At its best it represents a growth in economy, technology, and the ability to use the resources of the earth for the benefit of humankind. At its worst, it reflects a centralized system of control that exploits the earth and oppresses many of its citizens, an arrangement that rewards the rich and the powerful at the expense of the poor and the vulnerable. In the end, it is up to us to shape the future. We can only hope that we will optimize the benefits of civilization, while we strive to reform its more obvious elements of injustice.

THE IMPERIAL MIND AND STRUCTURAL VIOLENCE

Our popular assumptions regarding the benefits of civilization often fail to address its problematic side. We overlook what John Dominic Crossan describes as the "brutal normalcy of civilization."[3] What is this dark side of culture? In a word, it is the reality of *empire* as the primary form of civilization. Over the last decades there has been a flood of scholarly books on the significance of empire and its relation to human society.[4] An imperial form of government is the usual form that civilization has taken since its emergence following the Neolithic revolution. Crossan goes so far as to assert that "civilization itself . . . has always been imperial—that is, empire *is* the normalcy of civilization's violence."[5]

—

Obviously, not all social commentators would agree with this perspective. All the same, it is crucial to explore this oppressive side of empire. There is little doubt that massive changes are taking place in our contemporary economic and cultural arenas. The difficult part is trying to understand or interpret these developments. In their book *Empire*, Michael Hardt and Antonio Negri contend that the core characteristics of empire are an integral part of the newly emerging economic order.[6] While the colonialism of European dominance may be a past phenomenon, Hardt and Negri highlight the central elements of empire that appear in the growing trend toward globalization: new forms of racism, modern approaches to mind control, and fresh expressions of economic oppression. They also point to the power of transnational corporations and information technology as the tools that are defining a new "imperial global order."

In the social encyclicals of the past fifty years, including the recent *Caritas in Veritate*, by Pope Benedict XVI, the Catholic Church adds its voice to the concerns surrounding world markets, justice for the poor, and the need for a more just economic vision. In its myriad historical forms over the centuries, the system of empire has certain basic characteristics. By way of summary, we can point out the following:

1. Empire presupposes a *dominative,* hierarchical type of authority. The shape of this control has changed over the centuries, but some aspects of it can still be found in today's democratic forms of government.

2. An imperial approach takes for granted that there will be *inequalities* in the way resources are shared and access is provided. "The poor you will always have with you" is often a biblical proverb of justification for such an economic arrangement. The concentration of wealth in the hands of those who have power assures that there will not be enough to meet the needs of the poor and the disenfranchised.

3. An imperial form of government assumes—even requires— *enemies.* Civilization is not built solely on the arts, literature, beauty, and the promise of the good life; its imperial leadership also requires an atmosphere of insecurity, based on the fear and suspicion of the "other," in order to mobilize its citizenry.

4. This in turn demands that *war* be the normal instrument of promoting and protecting the structures of empire. In essence,

the ruling class tells its citizenry that for their protection the government needs to engage in ongoing military action.

5. There is also what might be described as a "theology of empire." Throughout history there has been a convergence of nationalism, patriotism, and religion. Caesar is divine and the king rules by divine right. Thus, depending on the historical era, the priestly caste or religious institutions often serve to legitimize the vision and practice of empire.

6. The fundamental goal of empire is peace through victory. But we should not be misled by the use of words. The peace that is spoken of here is the interval between wars. It is based not on cooperation but on competition, not on solidarity but on domination, not on détente but on triumph. This victory, in the standard imperial sense, will bring about peace (as in the *Pax Romana*), but it is peace through "justified" or necessary violence.

CONFRONTING THE ROOTS OF VIOLENCE

The relation between empire and civilization is ultimately grounded in another question. What are the social attitudes that create and sustain the "imperial mind"? The collective psyche that shapes human oppression is a theme that goes back as far as the ancient myths and the Hebrew Scriptures. It is also found in the Pauline letters and the confrontation of the early Christian communities with the Roman Empire:

> For our struggle is not against enemies of blood and flesh, but against the rulers, against the authorities, against the cosmic powers of this present darkness, against the spiritual forces of evil in the heavenly places. (Eph 6:12)

The author of the Letter to the Ephesians is not speaking here of power as we ordinarily understand it—as the capacity to act, to accomplish our goals, or to influence other people for good. He is talking about forces that are destructive, invisible, and hidden—so subtle, in fact, that we are often unaware of them. It is precisely because they are so veiled that they have the power to shape our attitudes and behaviors in ways that can lead to further systemic violence. We might think of them as the collective psyche of an institution or group that may be unarticulated but still operative as an ethical practice.

In ancient times these elements would have been identified as demonic forces or spirits. Obviously we continue to confront the reality of evil today, but we have come to recognize that these powers are not necessarily forces beyond our human experience that threaten to invade us, let alone "possess" us. They can just as easily be the inner momentum or "soul" of an institution or group in which we claim membership.

Few writers have helped us understand this phenomenon as clearly as the biblical scholar and peace activist Walter Wink. In his brilliant trilogy on power, he explores the ways in which political, economic, and religious systems are shaped by assumptions that embody and perpetuate human oppression.[7] In a recent book summarizing his previous work, Wink outlines what he means by the "Powers." He refers to them as the "corporate personality or ethos of an institution or epoch."[8] He also characterizes them as the "impersonal spiritual realities at the center of institutional life."[9] For example, they can be found in the collective attitudes of racism, sexism, militarism, exaggerated nationalism, materialism, consumerism, and classism. The overarching network of these diverse "Powers" constitutes what Wink describes as the "Domination System." It is characterized by "unjust economic relations, oppressive political relations, biased race relations, patriarchal gender relations, hierarchical power relations, and the use of violence to maintain them all."[10]

In themselves, the powers are not necessarily evil. The ethos of an institution, a nation, a social system, or an epoch can influence us positively or negatively. It can motivate us to an authentic spirit of generosity or it can manipulate us, consciously or not, into the further escalation of violence and injustice. Wink summarizes his view in simple terms:

> The Powers are good.
> The Powers are fallen.
> The Powers must be redeemed.[11]

What, then, is the task of those who pursue justice? First, they must read the signs of the times (Luke 12:54-56) by "*naming* the powers." This involves staying awake spiritually and bringing a critical perspective to our political, economic, cultural, and religious institutions. It also implies having the courage to break the silence and confront the structures of abuse. The second task is to "*unmask* the powers"—to reveal the economic, social, and psychological dynamics of oppression that are often hidden behind institutional rhetoric. Finally, it is critical to "*engage* the powers"—to struggle with them, not to destroy them but to redeem them; not to replace oppression with further oppression or to intensify violence with more violence, but to call these institutions back to their primal vision of service and the task of building justice.

SYSTEMIC VIOLENCE IN THE TWENTY-FIRST CENTURY

As insightful as this analysis is, it can easily remain distant from our experience unless we recognize the ways in which it is embodied in our world. Where do we see the powers or the domination system at work? In the nineteenth century the domination system was exposed in the practice of colonialism and slavery. In the twentieth century, we witnessed the horrors of totalitarianism as a tool of dictatorship and the mass control of millions of people. As we begin the twenty-first century, the long tolerated—and largely ignored—global violence against women is finally being exposed and confronted. In their sobering, yet hopeful book *Half the Sky: Turning Oppression into Opportunity for Women Worldwide*, Nicholas Kristof and Sheryl WuDunn reveal the brutality that women face, as well as their courage in overcoming thousands of years of systemic oppression.[12] The title of their book is taken from a Chinese proverb: "Women hold up half the sky." Women can rightfully claim this dignity and responsibility, but what the proverb proclaims is currently more of an aspiration than a reality. In widespread areas of our planet, girls are still uneducated and women are marginalized.

Half the Sky gives us shocking, personal accounts of young girls and women as they face terrifying forms of oppression ranging from forced prostitution, acid attacks, honor killing, and maternal mortality, to sex trafficking, mass rape, and other forms of "gendercide." In their writing, Kristof and WuDunn give us a striking example of what it means to "name" and "unmask" the powers of oppression. But they also call us beyond the violence to describe the courage and the resiliency of the human spirit. They are not simply giving us a list of problems; they are also outlining the ways that people are "engaging" the powers of oppression through education, social resistance, solidarity, and programs of opportunity. If the injustices that women suffer are the "paramount moral challenge"[13] of the twenty-first century, then there is also a parallel social, economic opportunity. There is a growing recognition on a global level—from the World Bank to the U.S. Joint Chiefs of Staff to aid organizations like CARE—that supporting the energy and gifts of women and girls is the most effective way to fight global poverty and political extremism.

One of the most dramatic examples of the emerging role of women is found in the work of Greg Mortenson and his commitment to "promote peace with books, not bombs," in remote parts of Afghanistan and Pakistan. In his earlier book, *Three Cups of Tea*, and more recently in *Stones into Schools*, Mortenson chronicles almost two decades of working with his nonprofit Central Asia Institute (CAI) to promote peace through education.[14] He and his colleagues have built more than 130 schools, most of them for girls, in regions of the world that have been largely illiterate and therefore vulnerable to political exploitation. The political and military "pragmatists" have yet to learn that the power of education is greater than an entire arsenal of nuclear weapons—and far more promising in creating a global community.

WALKING THE PATH OF JUSTICE

Most of us will probably not join humanitarian missions or become aid workers in third world nations. Nor do those nations and their communities necessarily want us to do so. If anything, they prefer that we get our lives on track and our ethical houses in order. In practical terms this means that we are called to name the sources of oppression in our institutions, to unmask the injustice in our religious structures, and to engage the violence in our political systems. If we take this task seriously, it will quickly erase the sentimental forms of spirituality that focus on personal satisfaction or fulfillment. It will clear away any illusion that religion is one more consumer product. This is a journey that is not found on MapQuest, since it is not exactly a tourist destination. This is not the road to social achievement or economic success. It is the way of the cross.

The only mentor who can help us understand this journey is the one who walked it in the first place. The turning point in the Gospel of Matthew takes place immediately after Peter acknowledges Jesus as "the Messiah, the Son of the living God" (16:16). As it turns out, Peter was correct in his affirmation, but badly mistaken in its meaning. He, like most of the other disciples, assumed that being the Messiah—literally, the "anointed one"—implied being called to political, military, and economic power. When Jesus told them that he must prepare to suffer, Peter "took him aside and began to rebuke him, saying, 'God forbid it, Lord! This must never happen to you.' But he turned and said to Peter, 'Get behind me, Satan! You are a stumbling block to me; for you are setting your mind not on divine things but on human things'" (Matt 16:22-23).

Setting our minds on human things, in this case, is an indirect way of saying that we tend to choose the way of dominative control. Whenever we assume, like Peter, that the call to leadership is a summons to fame and high-profile influence, it probably indicates that the "powers" have taken over our vision and our way of thinking.

In Luke's Gospel, the parallel moment arrives when Jesus tells his disciples that he must now face the suffering that accompanies the work of justice: "When the days drew near for him to be taken up, he set his face to go to Jerusalem" (Luke 9:51). To set one's face toward Jerusalem is a metaphor for naming, unmasking, and engaging the powers. Jesus, as the Letter to the Hebrews (6:20) tells us, is the "forerunner" (*prodromos*)—the one who exemplifies and embodies what it means to redeem human violence by exposing it and engaging it in order to transform it.

In practice, this implies a willingness to die to our learned cultural preference for control, to let go of the collective attitudes of racism, greed, gender bias, and homophobia, and other forms of prejudice. We do not die to the powers out of weakness or in order to "save our souls." We choose to become transformed in the face of these false and violent forms of control for the sake of God's in-breaking justice and solidarity. We make ourselves expendable, not because we are spiritual masochists or self-described martyrs, but for the sake of overcoming systemic violence. This is what Jesus meant when he said, "Those who try to make their life secure will lose it, but those who lose their life will keep it" (Luke 17:33).

5

Seeking Justice

The Emerging Biblical Vision

Naming God the liberator does not just craft one more symbol to add to the treasury of divine images. It puts a question mark next to every other idea of God that ignores the very concrete suffering of peoples due to economic, social, and politically structured deprivation.

—Elizabeth A. Johnson

The point of the pursuit of justice is not punishment but change of heart and reconciliation between people and between people and their God. The biblical symbol of justice is the river, not the woman with the scales.

—Terrence J. Rynne

I recently watched a news report regarding the execution of John Allen Muhammad, the man known as the Washington, D.C., Sniper, whose random shooting spree in the autumn of 2002 took the lives of ten people. After Muhammad was pronounced dead by lethal injection, a reporter asked one of the surviving family members: "Does it feel like justice was done?" Given the circumstances of this case, this is an honest question. If justice, as most people understand it in our culture, is to be carried out, it is clear that Mr. Muhammad deserved to die. I have profound empathy for the victims and their families, combined with a lingering bewilderment regarding the chaos that must have churned inside the perpetrator's mind. In the end, however, the reporter's question raises an even more complex set of issues. What is our understanding of justice? And how do we determine if justice was done?

Most people describe justice as having one's rights protected. They say it is about society being fair and getting what one deserves. Most of us can recall as young children occasionally telling our parents, teachers, or other caretakers, "It isn't fair." It appears that we have a deep, personal intuition about what is just. The difficulty is that what we think is obvious may not be quite as clear to others. Our instinct about justice may be unmistakable, but its application to particular circumstances is often confusing and litigious.

Over the centuries Christian teaching has articulated four types of justice. They are not so much differing definitions as they are four dimensions of one underlying ethic. We might picture it as a single ray of light radiating through a prism in four different directions, with each beam focusing on a particular context of social interaction. They can be summarized as follows:

- *Distributive justice* refers to what the wider community or society owes its individual members by respecting their rights and providing a fair allocation of life resources.
- *Contributive justice* focuses on our personal obligation to contribute to the wider society for the sake of the common good.
- *Commutative justice* is related to the obligations we have of being fair and respectful in our one-to-one relationships and business transactions with our fellow citizens.
- And, finally, *retributive justice*, or legal justice, refers to the rights and responsibilities of citizens to obey the laws of a society and to face the consequences if they refuse to do so.

There are four faces of justice, but our culture tends to focus on one of them. If we were to poll citizens in the United States or most other industrialized nations and ask them about their core convictions related to justice, it is likely that the majority would identify justice primarily, if not exclusively, with the last one listed—namely, *retributive* or legal justice.

POPULAR UNDERSTANDINGS OF JUSTICE

More often than not, we think of justice as protecting our rights, our possessions, and our personal safety. Consequently, our idea of justice is focused on creating laws, keeping laws, and punishing those who transgress them. The assumption is that those who transgress the law ought to pay the consequences. "You have to pay for your crimes," we say. True enough. This commonsense attitude underscores the societal need for impartiality. It reassures us that the rule of law is an essential step toward achieving social and political stability. Without a legal system and the capacity to enforce it, a society would teeter on the edge of anarchy, dictatorship, or political chaos.

For the average citizen, therefore, the purpose of the legal system is best symbolized by the familiar statue of Lady Justice, who is usually depicted as a blindfolded woman holding a set of scales in her left hand and a sword in her right hand. The statue of Lady Justice (in Latin, the goddess *Iustitia*) has its origins in ancient Hellenic, Roman, and early Egyptian concepts of law, where we also find the sources of our Western juridical philosophy. This image captures on a popular level what many people believe to be the essential characteristics of justice. First, we expect justice to be "blind," that is, detached from particular circumstances, people, and events, and focused instead on the principles and operative precedents of the law. Second, we demand that it be "evenhanded," that is, capable of remaining neutral and balanced in making legal decisions. Finally, the sword reminds us that justice should mete out punishment in accord with the seriousness of the crime committed.

The image of Lady Justice is an embodiment of retributive justice. It is the familiar icon that expresses our understanding of being honest and fair. We observe it as it is practiced in our courts and prison systems; we recognize it from classic western films; we read about it in the newspaper every day; and we watch it unfold on the evening news.

POPULAR JUSTICE AND THE BIBLICAL VISION

To what extent is this popular understanding of justice the same as the Bible's vision? Clearly, there are ways in which the familiar image of retribution overlaps with the biblical accounts. After all, the ancient Hebrew people shared much of the cultural heritage of their Near Eastern neighbors. From the outset, however, I want to highlight a core conviction. The central theme of these chapters is that retributive justice is *not* the leading edge, *not* the evolving vision of justice as it is articulated by the prophets and brought to fulfillment in the crucified and risen Christ. Rather, it is *restorative* or *transformative* justice—the commitment to solidarity with the poor and persecuted—that is the focus of biblical righteousness. This is the justice that is rising in the human spirit.

Using ancient biblical imagery, we can compare the evolution of justice to an olive tree. This revered plant grows slowly and has many branches, but the roots and the trunk carry the vital energy, the life sap. Likewise, there are several branches in the tree of justice. In these pages we are seeking the most authentic vision—the *taproot* that becomes the generative, life-giving branch—the branch that in turn flowers into the gospel and the challenge of creating peace in our contemporary world. For the sake of clarity and inclusion, we will first examine some of the other perspectives on justice. They are lesser branches, but their impact and lasting influence continue to shape our world.

THE BIBLICAL LANGUAGE OF JUSTICE

Justice is a central theme in the Hebrew and Christian Scriptures (as it is also in the Qur'an and the Islamic tradition). Its vision and practice unfolded over thousands of years in a worldview that is different from our own. It is a perspective that is less conceptual than dynamic, less abstract than grounded in the historical encounter between God and the chosen people. Within this history, there are two vital movements at work: first, the *meaning of justice is evolving;* second, *it evolves in a direction that is fulfilled in the life and ministry of Jesus and the radical demands of the gospel.*

The words for justice occur more than a thousand times in our sacred writings. In the Hebrew language the most common terms for justice are *mishpat* and *tsedeq/tsedaqah.*[1] In the *koinē* (common or popular) Greek of the Christian writings, we read of *dikaiosynē* and *krisis.* The term *mishpat* is usually translated as "justice" and *tsedeq/tsedaqah* is rendered as "righteousness." The term *tsedaqah* has an earthy, commonsense origin. It implies meeting a standard, or as we might say, "getting it right." Thus in the everyday language of Scripture a "righteous" weight is one that is in fact what the scale indicates it to be (Lev 19:36); a straight path goes in the right direction (Ps 23:3); and correct sacrifices are those that are not only performed according to the prescribed cultic rites, but also reflect a "righteous" heart on the part of the one offering them (Isa 58:1-14).

When we hear the word "righteous" today, the above images are not necessarily the first that come to mind. For contemporary people, righteousness usually refers to a form of personal integrity, or, in some instances, a false, hypocritical persona (as, in someone appearing to be "*self*-righteous"). Justice, on the other hand, is usually understood as something beyond the personal. It is more about the law and about the civic order that enshrines judicial principles and their administration.

In their general biblical usage these two terms (*mishpat* and *tsedaqah*) are used to describe the actual judicial procedure—the task of judges to administer the law carefully and fairly (Ps 1:5-6). Often these words are used interchangeably or combined in a poetic parallel. One of the most striking examples of this is found in Amos:

> But let justice [*mishpat*] roll down like waters,
> and righteousness [*tsedaqah*] like an ever-flowing
> stream. (Amos 5:24)[2]

This familiar passage gives us a clue to the developing understanding of justice. Clearly the prophet is speaking of more than the judicial system or a collection of laws. In linking justice and righteousness he is describing what we understand as *social justice* and its role in bringing protection to the poor and vulnerable. Already at this early phase, we see the emerging meaning of justice as liberation from all that holds people in bondage or oppresses their dignity.

JUSTICE AS LAW

For many people, the work of justice is a simple matter of creating and enforcing laws. If those who hold this point of view are also practicing Jews or Christians, they will likely further indentify justice with the Decalogue—the law of God given to Moses.

How accurate is it to identify biblical justice with this narrow juridical context? History gives us some evidence to support this perspective. The earliest collections of civil laws reach back to the late third millennium BCE in the ancient Near East. They come from places like Sumer, Egypt, and Babylon. The most famous of these collections, the Code of Hammurabi, appeared a few centuries later (approximately 1750 BCE) and has many features in common with earlier collections.

The Hebrew people, in their long transition from a seminomadic people to a more settled agricultural and urban population, combined elements from their early tribal customs with the civil laws that emerged from the early urban societies. These ancient collections of law are a fascinating source of study today. Since they arose in the same period of history and in a relatively small geographical area, they have common sources. Their language and legal directives reflect corresponding concerns about community and social interaction.

All the same, it would be a distraction, if not an outright source of confusion, to focus on these juridical parallels. There are similarities between the cuneiform laws of the early codes and the Torah, but there are also significant differences. Most of these arise from the dissimilar social settings of Mesopotamia and Israel. While Mesopotamian societies were agrarian, urban, centralized, relatively densely populated, and organized bureaucratically, Israelite society was located in the hill country, more pastoral, decentralized, kinship-oriented, and only mildly bureaucratic.

What is the understanding of justice in these early collections of laws? As noted above, these codes primarily convey the obligation to be *fair*. Their view of justice implies acting in an evenhanded way in one's everyday dealings related to the world of bartering, trading or purchasing food, clothing, and the materials necessary for shelter and safe travel—or in other words, with the everyday realities of being human. These civil laws deal primarily with the need for ordering economic relationships between people. They have many components that are still in use today, including a system of pricing, codified amounts of money for business exchanges, fines for wrongdoing, rules for inheritance, and laws regarding private property.

As down-to-earth as this approach appears, it also has its dangers. To begin with, it can easily drift into a shallow form of legalism. This occurs whenever we reduce justice to a simple matter of keeping the rules. To do so is to ignore the larger, more pressing issue of systemic violence. What happens, for instance, if the judicial system itself is unjust? What if it is dominated by the rich and powerful, who use the civil structures as a way of keeping the poor oppressed and their citizens without a voice? In the biblical context, laws—even those that are the most mundane and practical—have a wider scope than simply enforcing the current version of civil order. In the end, justice as civil law must be broadened to become a moral stance, an attitude of the heart that seeks to give everyone a place at the table. The preexilic prophets forcefully denounced the judges and kings who used their legitimate power in unjust ways to oppress the people, especially the poor and the vulnerable (Amos 5:7; 6:12; Isa 5:7, 23; Jer 22:13).

The entire Hebrew collection of law is referred to as the Torah, a Hebrew word that means "instruction or teaching." From one perspective the Torah is law in the same sense that the Code of Hammurabi is law. It is a collection of legal customs and practices that have been put into writing. It contains hundreds of rules, requirements, obligations, and punishments for offenders. Think again of the statue of Lady Justice—blindfolded, carrying scales and a sword. On another level, however, the Torah is quite different from civil law. Most law codes are written to be as exact and technically precise as possible. They need to be clear, comprehensive, and consistent. The less ambiguity there is, the better the system of law. This is because the principal audience for legislation—especially in Western cultures—is the legal establishment, whose task is to interpret and enforce the law.

This is not the case with biblical law. The audience here is not the professionals but the people—the entire community. In addition, the law is ultimately rooted in God—both as an attribute of the divine presence and as an ethical standard to be lived out by the people. The Torah is intended to be persuasive as well as regulatory. It is a call to conversion and commitment because it is grounded in the divine covenant, not just in human custom. It is, in short, an entire way of being and living in personal righteousness before God and in loving solidarity with the human community.[3]

JUSTICE AS PUNISHMENT

The worldview of the ancient people is different from ours, not just in terms of how they pictured the cosmos—the heavens above and the netherworld below—but also in their understanding of human behavior. The ancient stories and their descriptions of God flow from an anthropomorphic perspective. In simple terms this means that we often project our human emotions onto God. We also tend to read the events of life—both the catastrophic and the gracious—from our limited, often naïve view of cause and effect.

"Would it upset some almighty plan, if you made me a rich man?" This half serious, half playful question by the lovable character, Tevya, is a memorable line in the musical *Fiddler on the Roof*. It mirrors the unspoken assumption that somewhere there is a hidden design that the creator has put into the world. We not only look for a cosmic pattern; we also want to find a way to use this plan to our advantage. Generation after generation has tried to find the key to this secret, to discover a way to get God on our side.

The early Hebrews lived in a diverse cultural and religious setting. Most of the surrounding nations—Sumerians, Babylonians, and others—believed that the world was controlled by the gods, the forces of nature, or fate. The best anyone could do is to petition, placate, or appease the gods. More often than not this came down to waiting for the uncontrollable to occur. The Canaanite religions explained the mystery of punishment and suffering in terms of cosmic battles and conflicts among the gods. This is one of many dualist ways of explaining why catastrophes occur. Ultimately, dualism is a dead-end explanation for the way the world works. But over the millennia it has continued to attract followers, probably because it has a certain clarity and convenience about it. Thus, the painful times are blamed on the evil gods, while the years of prosperity are attributed to the benign gods. Mot, the Canaanite god of death, becomes the dumping ground for all forms of evil and human anguish, and Baal, with his consort, Astarte, is celebrated as the source of life, joy, and the return of spring each year.

For the Hebrew believer, the world was not in the hands of the gods, or fate, or evil forces that could plunge us back into chaos. God alone is creator, and the very act of creation, as we noted earlier, is a saving act, a liberating event. Unfortunately, monotheism does not solve the question of evil, suffering, or injustice. It only makes it more mysterious and puzzling. If there is only one God and that God is in charge of history, then somehow this same God is responsible for suffering and evil.

In the early stages of Israel's ethical consciousness, this is precisely the explanation that we hear. Instead of excusing their creator, the prophets argue that suffering does not escape God's notice. "I fashion the light and create the darkness," Isaiah says on behalf of God. "I make happiness and I cause misery" (Isa 4:7). Earlier the prophet Amos articulated a similar perspective in the form of a question: "Does misfortune come to a city if Yahweh has not sent it?" (Amos 3:6 [JB]).

Thus, one of the early explanations was that God punishes evil people and rewards the good. If you sin, you will face disaster in the form of some divinely imposed punishment. If you are righteous, you will in turn be blessed by God. "Misfortune pursues sinners," writes the author of Proverbs, "but prosperity rewards the righteous" (Prov 13:21). This view is also reflected in Psalm 1:6:

> For the LORD watches over the way of the righteous,
>   but the way of the wicked will perish.

The rhetoric of justice as punishment is woven throughout the Hebrew Scriptures. We are frequently reminded that God punishes sinners—both the individual wrongdoer and the nation as a whole for its transgressions. Everything from wars to natural disasters is interpreted in this cause-and-effect universe. Storms, fires, pestilence, floods, droughts, volcanic eruptions, earthquakes—all of these are perceived as God punishing the people—or their enemies—for their lack of obedience.

These anthropomorphic beliefs were alive and well in the time of Jesus. When the disciples of Jesus saw a man who was born blind they asked: "Rabbi, who sinned, this man or his parents, that he was born blind?" (Jn 9:2). Such beliefs still persist in our world today. Many biblical fundamentalists continue to believe that HIV/AIDS is a clear punishment from God for homosexual activity. These same religious commentators also understood the tsunamis in sub-Asia and the devastating earthquake in Haiti in the same simplistic manner.

CHALLENGING THE THEOLOGY OF RETRIBUTIVE JUSTICE

If we understand suffering as someone receiving their due punishment from God, we have, to put it mildly, an immense dilemma. "Theology," St. Anselm writes, "is faith seeking understanding." It is inevitable that good people will seek to understand the inexplicable. What kind of God allows or, in some mysterious way, causes indiscriminate suffering? What about the just people who suffer needlessly? And how do we explain the success and material prosperity of those who are blatantly unjust and who oppress the poor? If God punishes sinners, who are they? How do we distinguish the just from the unjust?

The poets of Israel understood the implications of these questions. They looked unflinchingly at the open wounds of human pain. They confronted the jagged edges of injustice all around them. They stared into the face of despair that waited, like a dark vortex, on the other side of their perplexity. Nonbelievers, when faced with suffering in the world, would simply find confirmation that "there is no God" (Pss 10:4; 14:1). Others could conclude that if God does exist it must be a God "incapable of knowledge" (Ps 73:11). The wife of Job pushes the argument to a final, desperate conclusion. She advises her beleaguered husband to "curse God" (Job 2:9).

The dilemma of faith that the ancient people confronted is no small matter. It is the central religious impasse, the haunting mystery that challenges a pilgrim people to encounter God in their dark night. This is the matrix that births the prophetic vision of justice, the crucible that transforms the vision of seeking peace and inclusion among peoples. In the face of this painful dilemma the prophets and poets were driven to find another way of understanding the meaning of God's care and compassion.

Between the sixth and fourth centuries BCE, an important transformation in the theology of justice-as-punishment began to take shape. It was initiated by the prophets' concern for the plight of the poor and the out-of-control excesses of the ruling classes. Their sense of outrage became identified with God as taking the side of the vulnerable and the marginalized. In their preaching these firebrands realized that the usual explanations for suffering were at best stumbling attempts to look for causes in the world of common sense. But their questions had moved well beyond common sense. This was a world of contradictions, where the old justifications for life's unfairness were no longer adequate. Soon they began to challenge the proverbial sayings that had long been proposed as "wisdom." Again and again they express their dismay at the prosperity of the wicked and the misery of the just. Ezekiel is one of the first prophets to attack the widespread assumption that suffering is a delayed punishment for the sins of our ancestors (Ezek 18:1–32).

This spirit of questioning became even more pronounced in the later wisdom writings, in what many scholars refer to as the "literature of resistance." This body of writing includes the poignant story of Job and the poetic musings of Qoheleth. Both of these books come under the general heading of wisdom literature, but they also reflect a significant evolution in the understanding of justice. They confirm what the earlier prophets had come to believe about God's advocacy for the poor.

FOCUSING THE VISION

We have explored some of the early and limiting understandings of biblical justice. At this point it might be helpful to summarize the main differences between our popular understanding of justice and the biblical vision.

- The biblical tradition of justice is not necessarily the same as the forms of justice that are practiced in our courts of law. Biblical justice assumes the necessity of the rule of law, but it transcends the practice of civil law. It has a different starting point than most popular understandings of justice.
- Our popular notion of justice is primarily an objective concept—it exists "out there" as an impersonal set of guidelines, a codified system of rules. It is established by the state and administered by the state's agents. Biblical justice is not in the first place a concept or a legal system. It arises not from a concern for law and order but from an encounter with the God of creation and liberation.
- Therefore, justice is, in the first place, something that God is and that God does. It is the divine initiative at work in history. In contrast to the assumptions that surround civil law, biblical justice finds its origins in God's initiative on behalf of the poor and marginalized. In the history of salvation, justice is revealed as God's passionate desire to stand at the side of the "little ones."
- The focus of biblical justice is twofold. First, it confronts the systems and agents of oppression that create structures of injustice. Second, its primary concern is the protection and restoration of the victims of injustice—the poor, the voiceless, the vulnerable.
- Biblical justice is inherently relational and focused on the common good. Over the years the intent of the law in many Western societies has become less concerned about the wider community and more directed toward areas of legal self-interest. As a culture we have been more interested in protecting individual rights, especially for those who have the financial ability to pay for legal counsel, than we have been committed to promoting social justice for those who do not have political or economic leverage.

- Biblical justice is not blind or neutral. It sees with the eyes of
  God. It feels with the heart of God. It is an urgent call to see
  the plight of the poor and to respond with passion and commitment. In this sense, we can say that God's justice is "tilted"
  in favor of those who are victimized by unjust social structures
  or whose voices are silenced by oppressors. Recent Christian
  social teaching has recovered this biblical vision of justice by
  emphasizing the "preferential option for the poor."

6

Avenging Blood

Primal Forms of Justice

*Evil is unspectacular and always human, and shares our bed
and eats at our own table.*

—W. H. Auden

On a bright April day in 1995, Julie Marie Welch, age twenty-three,
was one of 168 people killed in the Murrah Federal Building in Oklahoma City from a bomb detonated by Timothy McVeigh. Like all of
the other parents—and indeed the entire nation—her father, Bud,
was devastated by what had happened. All of his life he had been
opposed to the death penalty, but in the wake Julie's death he felt as
though his life and his convictions were falling apart. He went every
day to the site where Julie died. He lost sleep. His health began to
fail. Most of all, he felt his rage rising to the point where he wanted
McVeigh to be executed.

Then a series of events occurred that changed everything. A few
weeks after the bombing, Mr. Welch saw McVeigh's father on TV. "I
saw this big man, about my age," he recalled later. "He was literally
stooped over in grief. I felt like I knew everything he was feeling."
Eventually, Bud arranged to meet with Timothy McVeigh's father, Bill.
"I saw a deep pain in a father's eye, but also an incredible love for his
son. . . . I was able to tell him that I truly understood the pain that
he was going through, and that he—as I—was a victim of what happened in Oklahoma City."

Bud Welch began letting go of his anger. He slowly came to understand that executing McVeigh and his accomplice would be, in his
words, "an act of vengeance and rage . . . and that was why Julie and

167 other people were dead—because of vengeance and rage." In the end Bud Welch reclaimed the central conviction of his life: "It has to stop somewhere."

It has to stop somewhere. Who will help us end the cycle of revenge? We are informed daily that violence continues to spiral out of control. From wars to genocide, from honor killings to drive-by shootings, from political assassinations to gang murders, from domestic violence to state-sponsored terrorism, the fires of vengeance are continually stoked around the world. In the inner journey of Bud Welch and courageous men and women like him, we see violence reflected in the mirror of our lives. We step back from the image stunned. We wonder how they have found the spiritual resources to respond in a way different from that of so many generations of our fellow human beings. We catch a glimpse of the graced moments, the quiet, anguished transformations of the human spirit turning away from vengeance to compassion. We witness authentic justice rising.

In this chapter, we explore the roots of vengeance as it is described in the Scriptures. It has its origins in the first dawning of human memory; as early as the Genesis story of Cain murdering his brother Abel; as far back as the "avenger of blood" as a way of pursuing primitive justice; as long ago as the genocidal battles waged by Joshua in the name of God. Reflecting on this history enables us to understand the destructive power of revenge in our lives.

THE *GO'EL* AS AVENGER OF BLOOD

Prior to the Sinai covenant and the journey of the Hebrews to a more settled existence in what we know today as the Holy Land, the Hebrew people, like most of their contemporaries in the ancient Middle East, lived a tribal, seminomadic life. Their daily existence was demanding and dangerous. They lived at the brittle edges of life and death. Their survival depended on their communal efforts to protect the safety of the group. Tribal living was forged around the conviction that the entire community came from a common male ancestor and that its members shared the same blood. For ancient people *blood is the primal metaphor for life*—it is the dynamic force that sustains and binds people to one another, to the land, and to the responsibility of continuing the future of the tribe through offspring. For the people of that time, it was a simple, if dangerous, challenge: How do we sustain and protect what keeps us alive as a community—our shared life's blood?

In such a precarious setting, it was all but impossible to survive outside the bonds of blood and kinship. The commitment to solidarity in a tribe was paramount. It was also urgent that someone in the clan be responsible for protecting and sustaining the life of the community. Among the ancient Hebrews there arose the figure—and eventually the social institution—of the *go'el*, whose role was to fulfill this vital task.[1] The term *go'el* is usually translated as "redeemer," but it connotes a wide range of responsibilities related to protecting community life. The *go'el* was, in effect, the early justice maker, the one called to bring back the balance of life by protecting the vital interests of the group.

The etymological root of *go'el* is literally the "blood brother" or "next of kin." In the pre-covenantal era, when the Hebrew people were still scattered tribes, the *go'el* is described as having four different roles. Some of these duties continued long after the Hebrew people settled in Canaan and became a nation with judges, a king, and a collection of laws.

The first of these tasks was to be the "blood avenger" (*go'el ha'adam*). It was the responsibility of the next of kin to hunt down and carry out the death penalty on a person who had slain a member of the *go'el*'s blood relatives. This practice was by no means limited to the Semitic people. It was widespread in the tribal customs of most early cultures throughout the world. There are two factors that can help us understand this brutal ritual. First, we must remember the historical era in which this practice came into being. In the nomadic societies of the desert there were no police, no law or judicial system to defend the rights of an individual. Thus, the clan had to assume both the right and duty to protect itself. Second, even today, with an established rule of law, similar practices of vengeance exist in many civilized societies. It happens whenever people take the law into their own hands and pursue justice outside the legal structures. In the early tribal era, however, there were no laws, so the *go'el* functioned as a primitive form of deterrence. He also represented a means of bringing back "balance" to the invisible scales of justice—a time in which being alive was measured by the most basic life force: human blood.

When someone was killed in the early nomadic clans, the people would in effect say, "*Our* blood has been shed." Since the blood of the tribe was seen as one life-giving energy, all shared in it, and all were

responsible for protecting it. This ancient custom is expressed sav-
agely in the cry of Lamech:

> I have killed a man for wounding me,
>   a young man for striking me.
> If Cain is avenged sevenfold,
>   truly Lamech seventy-sevenfold. (Gen 4:23b)

Lamech was a descendant of Cain, who, after he murdered his
brother Abel, was condemned to wander in the desert. But Cain bore
a "sign," which, significantly enough, is not a stigma of condemnation
but a mark of protection and defiance—it indicates that he belongs to
a clan in which blood vengeance is carried out ruthlessly.[2]

At some point in their emergence as a people, the Israelites made
a significant step forward in their ethical awareness and practice. They
began making a distinction between accidental homicide and murder
(Exod 21:12-24). The so-called Cities of Refuge were instituted in order
to provide a setting in which the community could determine whether
a case of manslaughter was deliberate or accidental (Deuteronomy 19;
Numbers 35). If the elders of the city judged that the homicide was
intentional, the murderer was then handed over to the blood avenger,
who would take vengeance on him.

LEX TALIONIS—THE LAW OF RETALIATION

In humanity's early ethical evolution avenging blood often became
a vendetta that extended to the entire family of the murderer (see
Joshua 7; 2 Kings 9). We spoke earlier of the importance of understanding the different worldview from which this practice arose. This
is another example of an anthropomorphic way of interpreting social
ethics. The blood avenger was grounded in the firm belief that God,
in order to ensure the sacredness of human life, was the ultimate
Avenger and had determined the death penalty for murder (see Gen
9:5-6; Lev 24:17). In other words, the blood avenger was regarded as
the representative not only of the murdered man's family but also of
Yahweh.

The first step forward for the Hebrew people in their understanding of justice was to make a vital distinction between accidental homicide and intentional murder. A second stage was the development of

what is known as the _lex talionis_ (from the Latin, meaning "the law of retaliation"). To some people this form of legalized punishment sounds almost as primitive as the role of the avenger of blood. But in reality it is an attempt to keep the cycle of vengeance from spiraling into complete chaos. It also reflects the early judicial customs that began to emerge as societies moved from a nomadic way of living to developing villages and cities. The _lex talionis_ is expressed already in the Code of Hammurabi, but probably its most famous articulation is found in Exodus 21:23-25, ". . . life for life, eye for eye, tooth for tooth, hand for hand, foot for foot, burn for burn, wound for wound, stripe for stripe" (cf. Lev 24:18-21; Deut 19:21).

How can we consider this to be a step forward? Isn't creating laws for punishment only a way of sacralizing violence in the public sphere? It can be viewed as ethical progress because it moves revenge under the rule of law instead of leaving it up to each tribe or clan to carry out its own form of vengeance. At the same time, the _lex talionis_ carries forward the assumption that justice means punishment. Unlike direct retribution of the kind inflicted by the blood avenger, however, this law is administered by a larger corporate body—the village, the nation, or the state—that is intended to limit the revenge and to make it proportionate to the harm that has been perpetrated.

This, in turn, raises a further question: Was the _lex talionis_ as expressed in the biblical mandate of Exodus 21 intended to be taken _literally_? The scholarly debate around this question is apparently not fully resolved. It is clear, however, that the early judges of Israel—in the tradition of Talmudic law—interpreted these words figuratively. There are many contemporary Jewish scholars who believe that the literal interpretation of "an eye for an eye" was seldom if ever practiced, because it was never intended to condone mutilation. For them the _lex talionis_ is an example of what today we call "tort law." It should be interpreted as measure-for-measure or equitable redress for personal injury. It refers not to literal mutilation but to a different form of reparation. Their humane solution was to change retribution into monetary compensation. Working over centuries, in what we might image as a combined team of injury attorneys, medical experts, and spiritual counselors, they carefully designed a method of determining the value of physical damages, the cost of suffering, medical expenses, loss of income, and compensation for humiliation (today we would likely employ the term "emotional pain"). In a true sense, therefore, the Talmudic interpreters further developed the understanding of justice. They refined the notion of retribution by shifting it from physical retaliation to monetary compensation.

REVENGE IS SWEET, OR IS IT?

Revenge is sweet. This proverb originated with Homer in the *Iliad*, describing the way in which the vengeance of a warrior is stronger and more satisfying than the best honey. The desire to "make someone pay" is an emotional response that most of us recognize, if only in the secrecy of our hearts. Sometimes this sentiment can be as harmless as feeling good about yourself when you are proven right in an argument about facts or trivia. It might mean scoring an A on the big test, after your teacher told you that you may not have the capacity to grasp the material in his or her course. Sometimes we experience a certain sweet revenge in the world of sports—beating the team that trounced us last year at homecoming.

Often, however, it goes beyond healthy competition or letting off steam. Seeking revenge is an emotional drive—like lust or envy—that is often unspoken and unacknowledged, but functions as a powerful source of motivation. Corporate managers sometimes describe their careers in language that sounds like "it's just business," but often the desire to get even is one of the primal impulses hiding beneath executive ambition. Retaliation is not just a plot line for a Shakespearean tragedy. It is a subtext for many executive turnovers, as common as a business report.

Ernst Fehr, a behavioral economist at the University of Zurich, has been studying how our brains react when social norms are violated. In Fehr's research—a game involving monetary competition—two players are asked to exchange money according to various scenarios. When one player hoards the cash, the other has an opportunity to punish the offender. The player who lost money or was "short-changed" is hooked up to a brain scan while he or she is considering whether or not to retaliate. The results of the brain scan confirm what we know from observing ourselves and others. Fehr and his associates found that the part of our brains associated with feeling satisfaction was more strongly activated during the time that players contemplated getting even. "There is a hedonic force behind the punishment," says Fehr. Perhaps this is a euphemistic way of saying that we enjoy getting even, especially when it feels that we are

is this gendered? [handwritten marginal note]

engaging in "altruistic punishment" or we believe that we are uphold-
ing accepted social norms.[3]

There are serious scholars who believe that this instinctive
sense of "getting back" is a necessary, even a healthy dimension of
the human psyche, and that it benefits humanity as a whole. In his
book *Eye for an Eye*, William Miller advocates for this position.[4] He
maintains that the *lex talionis* was not, in the first place, a principle of
punishment, but rather a means of compensation for intentional and
accidental injuries. He attempts to rescue the legal tradition of retaliation from what he considers its "barbaric reputation" and to demonstrate instead that legally regulated revenge has helped the human
community achieve justice. For Miller and other legal commentators,
our language reveals an intuition about justice as restoring a measure-
for-measure balance. After all, we employ words that mirror a mer-
cantile outlook on life. We speak of payback, of owning up, of settling
accounts, and of getting even.

According to this perspective, there is even something of beauty
and grace about carrying a grudge to its successful conclusion. Why
else speak of "poetic justice" as though there is something aesthetic
about retaliation that is well executed? This fascination with revenge
is reflected also in the history of literature, film, and the popular
media. From the *Odyssey* to *Beowulf* to *Dirty Harry*, it is clear that the
human psyche is attracted by the notion of paying back an enemy or
the opposing side.

Given these attitudes, it is little wonder that the blindfolded goddess with the exact scales and the sword has become the most recog-
nizable symbol for justice in our culture.

While the *lex talionis* may indeed have been a step forward from
random blood avenging, I believe it is ultimately only a stepping-
stone along the way toward a deeper understanding and practice of
justice. Miller recognizes that talionic justice works better in honor
cultures, where there is a clear hierarchy grounded in patriarchy,
possessions, and power. In other words, in a highly controlled society, revenge can take on the appearance of being constrained and
measured. We can state it another way. Rage need not necessarily
be explosive or savage; it can also be cold, calculating, and efficient.
Viewed from the distance of history, these societies may appear to
be more functional and orderly. But are they truly just? The authentic test of justice is how the wider community treats its most vulnerable members.

In cultures of control, the rich and the powerful usually determine the structure and practice of civil justice, not the wider community of citizens. In hierarchical societies, the lower classes seldom have the resources to play the "honor game." Only the powerful have that privilege. Those without economic leverage—the poor, the orphans, the widows, the strangers, the women, the elderly, the mentally ill, the physically infirm, the sexual minorities, political and religious dissidents, to name only a few—do not have access to the system, or even a voice to raise in protest. Their continued presence itself is a silent cry for something beyond *lex talionis* as the road to justice. They tell us that justice needs to be more than revenge, more than payback. It must promote solidarity and give a voice to the voiceless.

SEEKING JUSTICE BEYOND RETALIATION

On an autumn morning in 2006, Charles Roberts entered a small Amish schoolhouse in Lancaster County, Pennsylvania, and shot ten young girls at point-blank range, killing five of them, before taking his own life. His last recorded words on the phone to the police were addressed to his victims: "I'm going to make you pay for my daughter." He apparently was referring to the death of his daughter (who had lived only twenty minutes) nine years earlier.

His family and neighbors were shocked and sickened by this unexpected outburst of violence on the part of Roberts. No one saw it coming. He appeared to be an ordinary hard-working family man who lived a quiet, routine life. He told no one about his plans. He said nothing about suicide or the arsenal of weapons that he had been stockpiling for a week. He left behind only a spiral binder with a checklist for terror. None of this can ever explain why an apparently devoted husband and father of three children would wreak such violence on people that he knew as his neighbors. We will probably never know the ultimate reasons that led him to choose such a brutal form of vengeance. Clearly, he was a troubled individual who carried an immense, smoldering rage inside of him, a form of resentment so deep that it became an obsession and finally a calculated plan of destruction.

If the actions of Charles Roberts are tragic beyond words, the response of the Amish community is inspiring beyond comprehension. Their immediate response was to reach out to the wife and family of the man who had murdered their children. Instead of the cry for vengeance in return, they supported one another in their desolation, mourned deeply and quietly, and extended a hand of support to the survivors of the perpetrator. The world stood in stunned amazement at such capacity to absorb violence without a spirit of retaliation.

Clearly, Roberts was a troubled man and his behavior an aberration. Perhaps one of the reasons that the story continues to haunt us is that we can recognize the desire for revenge even when we know that we would never act on it. *I'm going to make you pay*. In our truthful moments most of us have felt this or quietly said it to ourselves regarding some large or small hurt in our lives. Why do we want to make someone pay? For what are we seeking recompense? And even more importantly, what form of healing ever flows from taking revenge?

Jesus challenges the understanding of justice as retributive punishment and offers the radical alternative of nonviolent resistance and active love. There are other spiritual traditions that also believe in the surpassing power of compassion—that two wrongs do not make a right. They believe that retaliation is not only unethical but also impractical. It does not make things better. It only perpetuates a cycle of recurring violence. Even though it is demanding, the core vision of the Christian gospel is that it is better to confront, to call to accountability, and ultimately to forgive rather than to seek revenge when someone has been wronged.

In the Chinese tradition, the Taoist *wu wei* encourages the person who is wronged to accept the infraction and to take the least "resistive" action to restore interpersonal balance. Buddhism stresses the "weight of karma"—that cosmic life has its own way of restoring balance. A person might decide to make a retributive response to hurtful actions, but that act itself will have consequences. In the narrow confines of human experience it is likely that the suffering incurred by retaliation will come full circle, not only to the one who was the perpetrator but also to the individual who was wronged in the first place.

Just as there is an evolution of justice within the Judeo-Christian tradition, so there is also an unfolding of its understanding and practice in other religious traditions. The original meaning of *yoga* in the Subcontinent of Asia was yoking animals to be led into battle against one's enemies. With the development of Buddhism, this moved toward a different meaning of the *yogi* as one who battles with his or her inner resentments and anger in order to channel it into compassion. Similarly, the original meaning of *jihad* was, like the Christian Crusades, to destroy the infidel. But today Islamic scholars tell us that *jihad* has come to mean an inner struggle to overcome vengeance with compassion. It was the Indian Hindu Mohandas Gandhi who famously remarked, "If we continue to practice an eye for an eye, then the whole world will simply be blind." What all of these traditions appear to have in common is a core belief that the golden rule is the only way to overcome the cycle of violence.

In the history of Western civilization, we encounter a sad irony. It is not the teaching of Jesus but the earlier stages of ethical and legal thinking regarding retributive justice that became enshrined in our systems of law. In recent years, many prophetic people are reclaiming the gospel vision, but with much opposition from those who feel either that Jesus did not mean what he said or that it is only a personal ideal of behavior that was never intended to become part of our ethical practice.

7

Protecting the Vulnerable

God as Go'el

For your God is God of gods . . . who executes justice for the orphan and the widow, and who loves the strangers, providing them with food and clothing. You shall also love the stranger, for you were strangers in the land of Egypt.
—Deuteronomy 10:17-19

The recognition of the inherent dignity and of the equal and inalienable rights of all members of the human family is the foundation of freedom, justice and peace in the world.
— United Nations,
Universal Declaration of Human Rights, 1949

On the streets of Tehran, following the disputed election of June 2009, those calling for a recount and political reform took bravely to the streets. Among them—apparently by coincidence as much as by intention—was a young woman whose videotaped death became a global symbol in the struggle for justice. Moments before she died, Neda Agha-Soltan cried out, "I'm on fire!" Then blood gushed from her mouth. Her eyes drifted to the side and froze in stillness. She was dead. But her memory continues to inspire generations of women and men throughout the world who are committed to building a more just human community.

I'm on fire. Neda was likely struggling to describe the searing pain from the bullet in her chest. But her words have taken on a wider, more compelling meaning. She was also on fire with a passion for life and freedom, for human rights and dignity. Neda, and millions of women and men like her on this turbulent planet, are burning with a longing for justice. I only learned later that the name Neda in Farsi means "voice." Perhaps her death reflects another fierce truth: that millions of people are seeking to have their voices heard, their dreams pursued, their dignity honored, and their place at the table of life. The postmodern perspective tells us that history is a contest between competing narratives. If this is so, then the story of this young woman dying on the streets of Tehran has become a narrative of its own. It has captured the plight of women across our world. It has fired the human imagination to believe again in justice as a passionate commitment.[1]

In the face of tragedy, there is courage; in our chaotic world, there are resilient dreams of freedom stirring. The practice of justice as the path toward solidarity is germinating, as surely as spring, from the grass roots. From women's shelters to refugee camps, from the barrios of Central America to the mountain villages of Afghanistan, from the students in Tiananmen Square to the monks of Myanmar, from the women in the streets of Tehran to the members of the Peace Corps, from text messages in the Philippines to truth and reconciliation commissions in South Africa, the quiet, resilient work of peacemaking is unfolding.

Inner-city neighborhoods are standing up against the power of gang violence and asking for responsible measures of gun control. International religious and non-governmental organizations (NGOs) are providing rescue efforts, shelters, and job training for young women and children who have been trapped in the dark web of sex trafficking. Advocacy movements are demanding that criminal law move beyond the usual forms of retributive justice to models that are more restorative or even transformative.

What is this awakening energy? It is an emerging tide of hope, a song of freedom, a collective act of defiance. In the words of María Pilar Aquino, "Women wanted to define their own features, hear the sound of their voice, and feel the texture of their own skin . . . through hearing their own songs of joy and sorrow, they have found the 'coin' they had lost. They have recognized themselves as they are—Indian, black, mestizo, and white women involved in struggles, resistance and hope."[2] These are the sounds of justice rising.

THE EVOLUTION OF THE *GO'EL*

In the last chapter we explored the early attempts to pursue justice through the social institution of the *go'el*—the "kinsman"—whose role was to protect the safety of the community. The first responsibility of the *go'el* was to avenge the blood of someone who had been murdered in his tribal family or clan. In addition to the task of avenging blood, however, the *go'el* also had three other responsibilities:

1. If a family member was taken into *slavery*, it was the task of the next of kin to ransom or "redeem" him or her (Lev 25:47-49).
2. Likewise, if someone in the clan had to sell his *land,* it was the responsibility of the *go'el* to buy back the land rather than allow the family property to be lost (Jer 32:6-8).
3. Finally, if a man died without a male *heir*, it was the responsibility of his "blood brother" to marry his brother's widow so that the family name and blood line would be continued. The story of Ruth includes a tender—and more inclusive—version of this role of the kinsman.

Notice that the *go'el* functioned as a protector for the vital interests of the tribe—its lifeblood, its social solidarity, its land, and its future survival through offspring. These early practices of justice making were part of the unwritten ethical customs of people for centuries, perhaps even millennia. Why did they begin to change? The single most important event that reshaped Israel's encounter with justice is the exodus. God's gracious act of leading the community from slavery to freedom became the mobilizing metaphor for the Jewish people's relationship to God, with one another, and ultimately with other nations. It narrated a story of liberation and care for the vulnerable, and it raised persistent questions about retributive justice. Is avenging blood really the best way to protect the community? Or does it only generate further violence? Just as important, what about the people in the community who have no *go'el*? Who is the next of kin for those who have no one to protect them?

The Hebrew hospitality codes reveal how seriously the Israelite community took their call to reach out to vulnerable people. In the Book of Exodus the people are reminded that they must not wrong or oppress the strangers in their midst because once they were immigrants themselves in Egypt, and God chose to become their *go'el*—their next of kin or "redeemer" (Exod 22:21). The people are commanded not to abuse the widow or the orphan, for their cry—even if their oppressors attempt to silence it—will be heard directly by God (Exod 22:22-23).

There are two central questions, then, that challenged the Israelite people to re-vision their understanding and practice of justice. The first is related to those who need protection. Who should be included in the safety concerns of the larger community? Are there some groups who, because of their vulnerability and lack of status, deserve to have greater care and concern? The second question has to do with what it means to protect. Do we truly safeguard others by engaging in blood avenging—or its more refined version, retributive justice—as a form of deterrence? Is retaliation the most effective, ethical response to violence? In the context of covenantal faith, what does it mean to care for the vulnerable? These questions are ancient and disturbing. They are just as unsettling and perhaps even more urgent today.

The Exodus: Emerging Metaphor for Biblical Justice

The Pentateuch names three classes of people who are vulnerable and in need of protection: the widow, the orphan, and the stranger. In a culture that was slowly shifting from a seminomadic way of life to a more settled, agricultural and urban existence, these three groups of people had no *go'el*, no next of kin, to protect them. The memory of the exodus and its implications had taught the people that God chose to be their *go'el*—their redeemer and liberator—not because of their social status or political power, not because they were particularly intelligent or physically gifted, but out of the sheer freedom of gratuitous love. God chose to act because they were in exile and living as slaves. In that act of protection and liberation, the God of Israel was modeling a new meaning for justice and inclusion.

Let us look more closely at this event and its implications. When Moses encounters the presence of God in the burning bush, he hears these words: "Then the LORD said, 'I have *seen* the misery of my people who are in Egypt; I have *heard* their cry on account of their taskmasters. Indeed, I *know* their sufferings, and I have *come down* to deliver them from the Egyptians'" (Exod 3:7).[3] There are four verbs in this passage that reveal the seeking care of God, action words that also become vital descriptions for justice making: seeing, hearing, knowing, and acting. First, God *sees*—pays close attention to the suffering that is unfolding. Second, God *hears*—listens with compassion to the cry of the people. Third, God *knows*—which in the Hebrew language implies moving beyond empirical observance to an experiential understanding. Finally, God *comes down* to deliver—that is, God chooses to become present in an active way to liberate the people from their suffering.

This passage is a job description for justice workers. It names the interior stance of the heart, as well as the life-response of those who claim to believe in a God of compassion and equality. It challenges each of us to live our lives out of this vision. Contrast this scene in Exodus with the symbol of Lady Justice. The God revealed in the exodus is not a statue, not an abstraction, but a living, initiating, seeking presence in history. The God of the exodus is not blindfolded, impersonal, or somehow above it all. This is a God who sees, who hears, who knows, and who comes to liberate those who are in bondage.

God's seeking care and the exodus journey became a spiritual prism through which the people of Israel began to reinterpret their entire history. They remembered it not just as something that God did for them, but as a way that they, in turn, must be for others. Gradually, over the centuries, as they celebrated Passover, the people began to understand the implications of what had taken place in their lives. God's loving initiative on their behalf became, in turn, a summons to respond in a similar fashion toward others. It challenged them to ask difficult questions about their core ethical practices related to protection, family, relationships, justice, and the human search for *shalom*.

THE SABBATH AND JUSTICE

Genesis is the first book in the Hebrew canon, but it is not the earliest expression of Israelite theology. In the table of contents of the Hebrew Scriptures, we can think of this first book as the "introduction." This is usually the last thing an author or an editor writes. Thus, Genesis gives us a preview, a summary of the story of salvation that follows. It presupposes that the author or editor has already collected the body of writing and recorded the central vision. The final editors of Genesis are surveying the sweep of the Hebrew canon and seeking to encapsulate its meaning. We might imagine the editors looking over this collection of sacred literature and asking themselves: How shall we present this vision?

The most striking of these themes is that the God we believe in is a generous creator who desires all creatures to share abundantly and equitably in the community of life. This God—unlike the gods of surrounding nations—does not create by engaging in cosmic conflict. On the contrary, this is a transcendent God who is yet mysteriously present in the creative process. In calm serenity God speaks, and creation unfolds. The six days of divine creativity are portrayed in the form of a cosmic liturgy. Each of the six days opens with the introductory phrase "And God said." Thus, God's word is inherently generative; it brings forth what is spoken. Following this introductory phrase is a command, "Let there be . . . [light, firmament, sea/land, sun/moon, birds/fishes, animals/humans]." Each day also closes with what sounds like an antiphon of praise: "And God saw that it was good." On the sixth day after creating the woman and the man in the divine image, the author adds an adverb. God saw that it was "*very* good" (Gen 1:31).

The exodus event also provided the early Jewish sages with a way of rethinking the ancient creation stories and expanding the meaning of the Sabbath. Originally the Sabbath observance was linked to the Priestly account of creation and God's resting on the seventh day. The rationale was simple enough: "For in six days the LORD made heaven and earth, the sea, and all that is in them, but rested the seventh day; therefore the LORD blessed the sabbath day and consecrated it" (Exod 20:11). Thus, our Sabbath imitates and reflects God's rest. The Sabbath is a way of mirroring God's creative process in the rhythm of our daily lives. Like our creator, we spend our days working and then we "cease," which is the literal meaning of *shabat*. We labor and then we pause to be renewed.

It is easy to think of the Sabbath, as it is described in Genesis, as an afterthought. God had worked hard and deserved a rest. But if we think of the Sabbath merely as a "day off," we would be missing the point entirely. The Sabbath is the climax of creation, not its denouement. It is the radiance of being, not a postscript. The Sabbath reminds us that creation is rich, diverse, and abundant. It creates a holy space: "God blessed the seventh day and hallowed it" (Gen 2:3). It celebrates the beauty and lavish gifts of creation, an abundance that is to be shared, contemplated, and enjoyed—by *all*. *And it is precisely here that the Sabbath as rest encounters the Sabbath as justice.* In a patriarchal culture, where dominative power was the rule, slaves served at the behest of their masters. The Book of Exodus gives us the deeper reason for the Sabbath rest: "Six days you shall do your work, but on the seventh day you shall rest, so that your ox and your donkey may have relief, and your homeborn slave and the resident alien may be refreshed" (Exod 23:12). In the words of John Dominic Crossan, "The Sabbath Day was not rest *for* worship but rest *as* worship. It was a day of equal rest for all—animals, slaves, children and adults—a pause that reduced all to equality both symbolically and regularly. The Sabbath Day was about the just distribution of basic rest-from-labor as a symbol and reality of God's own distributive justice."[4]

The seventh day becomes a metaphor for God's loving care for all creatures, but especially for the vulnerable, the oppressed, and the marginalized. The continuity of the seventh day and its meaning as a time of equality and solidarity is reflected in the Torah in three striking ways. First, the human community is reminded that it does not "own" the land. For the Semitic peoples—whether in their lives as nomadic shepherds or in their more settled lives as semiagrarian people—the land itself is the source and symbol of life. Along with water and air, it is the most precious resource that God has given them. The evolving ethic of justice among the Hebrew people reflects this central value. The Book of Leviticus is unequivocal: "The land shall not be sold in perpetuity, for the land is mine; with me you are but aliens and tenants" (Lev 25:23). The earth is ultimately not the possession of any human individual or group, but belongs to God's plan for abundance and just distribution: "The earth is the LORD's and all that is in it, the world, and those who live in it" (Ps 24:1).

The second instance of the Sabbath-as-justice is found in laws related to ordinary business transactions and the everyday tasks of making a living. The concern to maintain God's vision of abundance and restorative justice is expressed in laws that forbid interest on loans and the careful guidelines surrounding collateral in business transactions. It is made even more specific as these sabbatical laws are applied to forgiving debts and freeing slaves. Always the emphasis is that creation belongs to God, who first shaped it and shares it abundantly with the creatures of the earth. Human beings are tillers of the soil and keepers of the garden. Our "dominion" is one not of exploitation but of stewardship: the care of the earth's gifts and resources.

The third, and in some ways the culminating high point of God's sabbatical vision, is found in the eventual practice of the Sabbath year (every seven years) and beyond that in the practice of Jubilee (every fifty years). These are all ways in which the people strove to limit the incremental forms of injustice and social inequality and to envision a world of mutuality and *shalom*.

WHO ARE THE VULNERABLE TODAY?

The descendants of Abraham and Sarah, Isaac and Rebekah, gradually came to understand a more expansive meaning of justice, not as vengeance or retribution but as solidarity with the vulnerable. It can be summarized in this paraphrase of the biblical mandate: *You must*

not molest the widow, the orphan, or the stranger, because when you were
vulnerable and in need, I was your go'el, your protector and liberator.

The prophets echo these same themes by confronting the political
and religious structures that exclude and oppress those most in need.
Jesus expanded these categories of vulnerability in his time by, in
effect, saying to the religious leaders and people: You must not molest
the blind, the lame, the leprous, the imprisoned, the ritually unclean,
or the mentally ill. You must not look down upon women, tax collec-
tors, Samaritans, or others who are different from you. You must feed
the hungry, give drink to the thirsty, welcome the stranger, clothe the
naked, care for the sick, and comfort the imprisoned (Matt 25:31-46).
In the Beatitudes, which summarize this justice tradition, Jesus tells
us that the vulnerable are blessed. Ironically, he also tells us that they
are a challenge and a blessing for the rest of the human community.
Those who are poor, those who mourn, those who are humble like
the earth, those who hunger and thirst for justice, those who mourn
for the wounded in spirit, those who are compassionate and create
peace in their daily lives, those who are persecuted because they stand
against the night of oppression—all of these Jesus holds up not as
victims but ultimately as victors over the systems of oppression.

If the authors of Exodus were naming the vulnerable today, whom
would they include? If the prophets were speaking of those who need
the special care and protection of the wider community, whom would
they name? If Jesus decided to update his mission statement at the
synagogue at Nazareth (Luke 4), or if he reframed the Beatitudes for
our age, whom would he add to his already extensive list? To whom
would he reach out with compassion?

We can only assume that the following groups—among others—
would be included: those who are victims or survivors of genocide and
ethnic cleansing; the refugees of war; the children dying of starva-
tion or HIV/AIDS; the poor who cannot afford health insurance for
themselves or their children; the homeless and the forgotten; undocu-
mented immigrants and their families; the victims of domestic violence; the elderly poor who have no family to support them; sexual
minorities who are given the message that they do not have a place
at the table of God; persons living with chronic illnesses; the physically and developmentally challenged; persons living with Alzheimer's
and their caregivers; cancer patients and those who care for them; the
mentally ill who live with social stigma each day. And so many others
that often remain unnamed in our society.

There is another group of vulnerable people who, I believe, would find special concern and a singular response from the crucified and risen One as he is present in the human community today. It is not that they are newly arrived on the scene of history, for they have long been part of the invisible, underground world of oppression. Until recently, however, the horrifying reality of their suffering has largely been kept secret by the tangled web of violence that exploits them. I am speaking here, of course, of *victims and survivors of sexual abuse*.

Alice Walker's novel *The Color Purple* is the story of the young woman Celie and her search for healing in her life. The opening words of the book relive the scene in which Celie is raped by her stepfather, followed by his stern warning: "You better not tell nobody but God." So Celie turns to the only safe presence left in her life. In a series of letters that become the literary framework for the novel, she tells her story to God. She recalls that when she cried out in pain, her stepfather choked her and said, "You better shut up and get used to it." Celie writes, "But I don't never get used to it."[5]

For as long as human beings can remember, vulnerable people, most of them women and children like Celie, have been told by their abusers and by unjust social—and often religious—systems to "shut up and get used it." And for just as long, most of the victims had only their own broken hearts and God to whom they could turn. For many of them, God was simply one more silent, distant presence—or perhaps more correctly, one more *absence*. Sexual violence is the silent scream in the recurring nightmares of humanity; it is the multitude of invisible faces hidden in the canvas of recorded history.

In our emerging global cultures, sexual abuse continues to be a tragic way of life for millions of women and children around the world. It is the predictable aftermath of wars and revolutions; it is taken for granted as an instrument of political and military strategy. It is a social reality in impoverished countries, where families sometimes sell their young daughters into prostitution for economic survival. But it is also the unspoken reality in many middle-class and affluent families in industrialized countries. In recent decades sexual violence has become increasingly graphic and explicit. Physical brutality is explicitly linked to pornographic images that reduce persons to their body parts, turning them into objects of rage, lust, and brutality. Interpersonal violence is an equal opportunity perpetrator. It is not limited to any national identity, economic class, racial category, or religious preference.

Recently I watched the film *Fields of Mudan*.[6] It is a heart-wrench-
ing story of a young girl trapped in the vicious web of sex trafficking.
In viewing it, I was literally moved to tears. It is one thing to read the
sobering statistics surrounding this global tragedy. It is another to
see this reality portrayed with such poignancy on the screen. The film
is a fictional narrative, but viewing it creates a profound emotional
impact. It puts a face on statistics. It makes real the experience of
millions of young women for whom this is not fiction but a terrifying
way of life. The only solace Mudan finds is the fields that she creates
in her imagination. They function as a form of psychic dissociation—a
place of refuge that gives her comfort and the inner strength to keep
going. This intentional, wakeful dream, together with the memory of
her mother, is her anchor of hope. Mudan also develops a close friendship with Faye, another young girl in the imprisoned community. But
their bond of support cannot keep them from the shameful violations
or the horrific suffering that both of them must eventually endure.

The contemporary world has named the crime of sex trafficking
for what it is: *slavery* and *torture*. It is tragic that it has taken Christianity almost two millennia to condemn slavery. But slavery did not
end with the Emancipation Proclamation in 1863. Nor did it cease with
the Universal Declaration of Human Rights by the United Nations in
1949. If anything, slavery—preying on innocent children and young
women in particular—has increased in these intervening years. It is
estimated that almost thirty million slaves exist in our world today,
more than at the height of the European/American slave trade in the
eighteenth and nineteenth centuries. Girls and boys from as far away
as Southeast Asia, Africa, Central America, and Central Europe are
being bought and sold into the underworld of the human sex trade.

Not all of them are hidden in dark basements or in shadowy, back-
room prisons, however. In the United States, trafficking victims are
often invisible even though they are working in public settings such
as restaurants, apparel manufacturing, hotel service, construction, or
agriculture. Psychologically and physically they are forced to present a
"normal" social persona, but their inner lives are broken and unspeak-
ably violated.

JESUS: PROTECTOR OF THE VULNERABLE

The vital connection between sexuality and power, love and justice,
has until recently been largely ignored by most Christian traditions.

Over the centuries, the churches have had a great deal to say about sex, but not as much about the misuse of power. On the other hand, the Jesus of the Gospels does not say much about sex, but he speaks out clearly against the abuse of power, violence, and the need for loving, mutual, and respectful relationships.

If biblical justice is God's passionate desire to stand at the side of the 'anawim (the vulnerable people in our midst), then Jesus embodies the frontier of this compassionate quest. Jesus is the go'el for all of humanity, but especially for the vulnerable and the oppressed. In the writings of the Johannine tradition, Jesus speaks of himself in two related images of protection and justice making. He describes himself as the gate for the sheepfold *and* the shepherd who gives his life for the flock. In ancient Palestine, as night was falling, the shepherd on duty would gather the various flocks into a natural enclosure and then position himself as both the sentinel and the gate to this enclosure. In this latter role, Jesus describes his mission in these striking words: "I am the gate. *Anyone who enters through me will be safe*: such a one will go in and out and find pasture. The thief comes to kill and destroy. I have come that they may have life and have it to the full" (John 10:9-10 [JB]).

Anyone who enters through me will be safe. I no longer read these words without hearing them in the context of God's liberating justice—the compassion that seeks to protect the vulnerable against those who would exploit them. In the context of our contemporary concerns regarding sexual abuse and domestic violence in families, as well as our growing confrontation with misconduct in professional and ministerial settings, this passage is a striking metaphor for biblical justice. The first task of a believer—whether he or she is a parent, a business executive, an elected political leader, a professional helper, or a career minister—is *to create a safe place for relationships*. This is a particularly urgent responsibility when those involved in the circles of our care are children or vulnerable adults.

In the Gospels, the role of protecting the vulnerable is the clear focus of Jesus' ministry. This is not a negotiable piece of legislation. It is not a responsibility that we can avoid by appealing to attorneys, insurance companies, or bankruptcy. The gospel mandate to advocate for those who are at risk is clear and unambiguous. If we, as communities of faith, do not choose to stand by this vision, who will?

8

Bearing the Pain of Others

The Servant of Justice and Peace

> *And yet ours were the sufferings he bore,*
>   *ours the sorrows he carried.*
> *But we, we thought of him as someone punished,*
>   *struck by God and brought low.*
> *Yet he was pierced through for our faults,*
>   *crushed for our sins.*
> *On him lies a punishment that brings us peace,*
>   *and through his wounds we are healed.*
> —Isaiah 53:4-5 (JB)

In 1959, André Schwarz-Bart published his novel *The Last of the Just*, a moving account of a young Jewish man, Ernie Levy, and his journey through the hell of Nazi Germany.[1] The narrative begins by describing the persecution endured by the Levy family going as far back as twelfth-century England. Thus, the author inserts his story into the ancient Jewish legend of the *lamed vov-niks*, the thirty-six "just ones" in each generation who bear in their lives the suffering of the world. For over eight centuries the Levy family had given over a *lamed-vov* to God. In 1933, as Hitler seizes power, it is Ernie Levy who is destined to become the "last of the just."

According to the Jewish Talmud, this revered tradition of the righteous persons (*tsaddiqim*) dates as far back as the time of Isaiah. The righteous ones, in the depth of their being, live out of the divine presence, and thereby keep the world from collapsing. No one knows who they are. They themselves, because of their humble, generous stance of heart, are also unaware of being chosen for this demanding role.

But through their willingness to take on the brokenness of the world and to carry the pain of others, they somehow assist God in moving history forward.

The *lamed vov-niks* embody the emerging vision of justice that we are describing here, a presence of solidarity that transcends theologies of vengeance and retribution. Their lives are rooted in *tsedaqah* and *tikkun olam*—literally, *righteousness* and the *healing of the world*. This sacred legend in the Talmud serves as a metaphor and a threshold for the themes in this chapter.

THE MYSTERIOUS SERVANT OF ISAIAH

In the book known as Second Isaiah (chapters 40-55 of Isaiah), there appears a person of justice called the *'ebed Yahweh*—the servant of the Lord. This figure is unprecedented in biblical literature and represents a leap of ethical consciousness in the history of salvation. We come to know this faithful servant through a series of four poems: Isaiah 42:1-4; 49:1-6; 50:4-9; and 52:13-53:12.

The servant is mysterious, challenging, and evocative. In Isaiah's literary style the servant is depicted as male. For reasons that will be addressed below, I believe the servant is an archetype of any person—male or female—who is willing to bear the pain of others in courageous service. For this reason, I choose to use gender-inclusive language in speaking of the *'ebed.*

At one level the servant integrates many of the features of past religious leaders in Israel. For example, she has the classic qualities of a prophet. She is called by God and gifted with the Spirit (42:1). She speaks out courageously, but does not shout or threaten in the language of retribution (42:2; 49:2). She is sent to teach all peoples about the ways of God (50:4). She also embodies many of the traditional qualities of a judge or a king: she pronounces judgments grounded in spiritual insight (42:3); she is a pathfinder, and a wisdom figure who offers liberation to the nations (49:6).

The servant is prophetic and regal, challenging and wise; and yet the *'ebed* is more than any of these qualities. It is almost as though the author of Isaiah is searching for a new term to describe a different way of being faithful and just. None of the past models of leadership is adequate to describe his mission. Perhaps this is because, in the servant of Isaiah, a new and deeper dimension of spiritual consciousness is emerging. This rising awareness is embodied in the role of *redemptive suffering* as a way of enfleshing justice and creating peace. The servant pursues justice and *shalom* not by the military power of a David or by the prophetic vengeance of an Elijah, but by offering his life as a gesture of healing—an embodied "bridge over troubled waters." He seeks to bring about *shalom* through the self-gift of his life in overcoming violence.

THE SERVANT OF HEALING JUSTICE

Who *is* this servant? The literal meaning of *'ebed* in Hebrew is slave. In sociopolitical categories the term refers to a person who is under legal obligation to obey a master. In ancient Israel the terms "slave" and "servant" were often used interchangeably. Servants were usually slaves, which in essence meant that they were the property of another person and completely at that person's disposal. In the spiritual meaning, servants of God were prominent leaders or intermediaries between God and the people. Moses, Miriam, Joshua, Deborah, David, the prophets, and even Israel collectively are called servants of God.

But the title "servant of the Lord" takes on a more profound meaning in the context of Second Isaiah. Scholars still debate whether these songs were written independently and then incorporated into the text, or whether they are an integral part of this author's writing and vision. There is a similar disagreement about the identity of the servant. Based on the second poem (49:3) some have interpreted the servant as representing collectively the Jewish people in exile—the faithful remnant. Others look for an individual person, including the unidentified poet himself/herself, or other historical figures such as Hezekiah, Josiah, Zerubbabel, Cyrus, Ezekiel, Moses, or Job.

My conviction is that the servant does not refer to an actual historical figure. Nor does the *'ebed* necessarily point to the collective or ideal Israel. Rather, the servant is an emerging archetype in the religious consciousness of Israel, not unlike the Talmudic tradition of the *lamed vov-niks*. The servant of the Lord, in short, reflects a movement beyond justice as vengeance or retribution and instead embodies justice as a restorative, healing power.

The first of the servant songs (Isa 42:1-4) describes the *'ebed* as being anointed by the spirit of God to bring "true justice" to the nations. It is not her mission but the manner in which she is to carry it out that reveals an entirely new meaning of justice. The servant stands in sharp contrast to the earlier tradition of military leaders and kings of Israel, who are portrayed as being sent by God, and in the name of God, to destroy the enemies of Israel. This servant will bring about true justice not by vengeance, not by violent victory, but by bearing undeserved suffering on behalf of the community.

Perhaps the author of these four songs in Isaiah has chosen the term "servant" precisely because this role breaks the boundaries of past perspectives. The work of the servant reaches its climax in the fourth song (52:13-53:12). In this passage—familiar to Christians from the readings on Passion Sunday and Good Friday—the servant carries out a role that no other charismatic figure in Israel has taken. He freely chooses to confront and carry the hatred and violence of others for the sake of healing the brokenness of his community. In stark contrast to the earlier role of the *go'el* as avenger of blood, the *'ebed* seeks justice not through violent retribution but through redemptive suffering. *Instead taking the blood of others to restore some cosmic balance, the servant gives his/her own blood to achieve authentic peace.*

In the earlier history of Israel, as we have seen, justice had a strong component of vengeance. The *go'el* restored the "balance of life" by avenging the blood that had been taken from his tribe or clan. Gradually the task of the *go'el* was expanded to other life-affirming and protecting responsibilities in the community. His role as avenger of blood became limited through the *lex talionis*. We can trace a historical thread between the *go'el* and the *'ebed*, but there is also a theological disconnect—a breakthrough to an entirely different understanding of how to bring about justice and the flowering of peace.

HISTORICAL ROOTS OF THE SUFFERING SERVANT

The early Christian community saw Jesus of Nazareth as the fulfillment of the mysterious figure in Second Isaiah. But before we explore how this is realized in him, it is important to look back, seeking to understand where and how such an archetype could emerge in the history of Israel. What caused Israel's religious consciousness to shift from the earlier understandings of justice as vengeance or retribution to justice as nonviolent solidarity? There are three significant reasons for this leap forward in ethical thinking: the encounter with suffering;

the challenge of inclusion; and the emerging concern for victims of violence.

The Encounter with Suffering

In 587 BCE, the Babylonians conquered Jerusalem, leaving widespread devastation in their wake, including the destruction of the temple, Israel's central religious symbol. Thousands of Jewish survivors were taken into exile in Babylon. This event shook Israel's faith to it depths. It left many wondering if God's promise to them had been only an empty illusion. The suffering of the people was widespread, and many of the Hebrews despaired or turned to other religions.

However painful and humiliating the exile was, it also carried an invitation to conversion. During those dark years a deeper, more purified faith began to emerge. The prophets had spoken often of a "remnant" that would remain faithful to God and to the desert covenant. During the exile this scattered group of disciples came into being—a small politically insignificant community of refugees who trusted in God even in the face of adversity. They are remembered as the 'anawim—the "little ones" or the humble followers of the living God. Zephaniah speaks of them in these terms:

> . . . I will remove from your midst
>   your proudly exultant ones,
> and you shall no longer be haughty
>   in my holy mountain.
> For I will leave in the midst of you
>   a people humble and lowly.
> They shall seek refuge in the name of the Lord—
>   the remnant of Israel. (Zeph 3:11b-12)

Suffering can either make us bitter and cynical or, as in the case of Israel's remnant, it can invite us to "seek refuge in the name of the Lord." This is about perseverance, not flight. It is focused not on avoiding pain and loss but on how we respond when these realties assault our lives. Perhaps we can put this in a more practical framework. Most of us do not have to seek out the cross. It has a way of finding us in its own time and on its own terms. Zorba the Greek, in Nikos Kazantzakis's novel of the same name says it well: "Life is trouble, only death is not." Ironically, this sobering commentary finds a parallel but different perspective in the words of Jesus: "In the world, you will have trouble, but be brave; I have conquered the world" (John 16:33 [JB]). What both the fictional Zorba and the real Jesus acknowledge is that to be human is to live with the daily reminders of our mortality. There is no free way around Calvary, no good news that is not also demanding news. For most of us trouble is a given. The difficult part is choosing to be brave and, even more so, trusting that suffering love can indeed overcome the world.

Can we truly rely on this possibility? Can redemptive love—a life given in nonviolent service—actually "conquer" the world of violence and injustice? It took our forebears in faith centuries of suffering to begin to grasp the possibilities of this emerging vision. I am not speaking here of the "normal" ways that we experience the brittle edges of finitude. I am not referring to natural disasters, sudden illness, financial crises, the early demise of our loved ones, or the daily struggle against the odds of life. These represent sufficient "troubles" to make most of us discouraged, or at least a bit weary. They can be overwhelming, but, given the human condition, they are not wholly unexpected.

In this case, I am addressing something more challenging and disheartening, namely, the suffering that we inflict on one another because of fear, jealousy, ignorance, or hatred. In most instances, the deepest cause of human desolation is the violence that individuals and groups of people perpetrate, often in the name of God, on their fellow humans. It is this encounter with suffering at the hands of others that ultimately transformed our understanding of justice.

The Challenge of Inclusion

The Israelites' self-understanding as a nation was grounded in the conviction that they were God's chosen people. To be the "elect of God" is a great honor, but it also comes with an immense responsibility, and it carries perilous temptations. If you are chosen, you are exceptional and privileged, perhaps even unique. The people chosen by God thought of themselves as a people set apart. They were different from the other nations because of their covenant with God. They were distinctive in their worship, their vision, and their ethical practices. The Book of Leviticus, with its laws of ritual purity, reflects the original meaning of holiness (*qadosh*), which implies being apart from others and participating in the transcendence of God.

If you are different from other people, there is a quiet temptation to think that you are also *better* than they. This, in turn, leads to a subtle form of arrogance. If God has chosen us, it is because God is on our side and will continue to take our side against the "others." The prophets spoke out strongly against this attitude of national entitlement. They criticized the haughty lifestyle of the rich and the powerful. They raised their voices against the self-righteousness of the priests, and they condemned the court prophets who assumed that God would automatically be on their side in time of war. Speaking on behalf of God, Amos offers a stark reminder:

> You only have I known
>   of all the families of the earth;
> therefore I will punish you
>   for all your iniquities. (Amos 3:2)

The collapse of national sovereignty and the heartbreaking sojourn of the exile purified Israel's claim to exclusivity. But it did not remove it altogether. Some scholars believe that the emergence of monotheism and its parallel belief in election actually exacerbated the fear and suspicion of the "other" by creating an "us versus them" mentality that inherently leads to an overzealous nationalism.[2] Obviously, Israel is not alone in wrestling with the challenge of an overinflated collective identity. This, it seems, is the perennial struggle of humanity, as we seek ways of living with diversity and, at the same time, respecting the dignity of others. In the pursuit of civilization, we slowly evolved from fierce tribal loyalties, only to become warring nations, still suspicious of others, still competing for resources, and still trapped in the illusion that we are better than other ethnic groups. The challenge facing the human community today is whether we can become a workable global community before we destroy ourselves or devastate our environment—or both.

In the figure of the *'ebed Yahweh* we encounter a mysterious paradox. On the one hand, the theme of election is accentuated with even greater clarity. The servant is neither a king nor a priest, nor a prophet, since each of these is chosen from among the living community. These persons receive their calling as they grow toward maturity and then are anointed for their mission. But the servant hears God's call in his mother's womb and his name is given directly by God (Isa 49:1). His entire existence and mission are dependent on the divine initiative. The servant's call is directly related to God's passionate desire to reach beyond national borders to the wider community of humankind:

> It is too light a thing that you should be my servant
>> to raise up the tribes of Jacob
>> and to restore the survivors of Israel.
> I will give you as a light to the nations,
>> that my salvation may reach to the end of the
>> earth. (Isa 49:6)

It is essential to honor both sides of this creative tension. The *'ebed* is indeed chosen, but she is called to solidarity, not separation. She is anointed not for exclusion but for the inclusive service of all people, the encompassing task of liberating others from oppression. She is called not to privilege or entitlement but to carry the violence and brokenness of humanity toward healing and true *shalom*.

Advocating for the Victims

The postmodern perspective tells us that history is written by the winners. It also reminds us that the victors narrate the story according to their self-interest. It should not surprise us, then, that over the millennia the victims of violence have been largely hidden from view. They are the invisible threads in the tapestry of history, the silent faces in the human crowd. Victims are not only hidden; they are frequently vilified as "sinners" and blamed for society's problems. They become the scapegoats for the powerful and successful, including those who consider themselves religiously and ethically righteous.

From the beginning of human civilization, there is evidence of what we can only describe as a collective persona of respectability. It goes by many names, including ambition, heroism, initiative, and the entrepreneurial spirit. But beneath this lofty rhetoric there is often a distorted form of human craving. This is what René Girard has characterized as "mimetic desire"—the tendency to distort relationships through the prism of social jealousy and enmity.[3] Thus, competition easily leads to suspicion, suspicion leads to projected fears, fear leads to "justifiable" rivalry, and the confluence of all of these leads to violence.

Some commentators tell us that we find a similar pattern in the Jewish and Christian writings. After all, they would argue, the Hebrew Scriptures begin with a fratricide and move rapidly toward the scattering of the nations, rivalry around national identities, and holy wars to conquer new lands—all of this with the apparent intention and blessing of God. This is a concrete description of what Girard calls "sacralized violence." But if there are similarities to other cultural practices and historical narratives, there are even more astounding differences. The Jewish texts, starting with Cain and Abel, gradually begin to dissociate God from approving or participating in human violence. Instead, the *victims* of violence become the concern and eventually the passionate focus of God's liberating love. They become visible. Their voices cry for justice in the night. The servant of the Lord is a major stepping stone in this shift toward unveiling violence and advocating for victims. Instead of making brutality something culturally respectable and religiously justified, the servant freely chooses to confront the violence and transform it into healing service.

JESUS AS THE SUFFERING SERVANT

The Christian writings identify Jesus as fulfilling the role of the *'ebed Yahweh*. At his baptism Jesus hears echoes of the first servant song: "You are my Son, the Beloved; with you I am well pleased" (Mark 1:11; see also Matt 3:17; Luke 3:22). As the blind, the lame, and the broken come to Jesus, Matthew explicitly links Jesus' ministry to this same passage:

> This was to fulfill what had been spoken through the
> prophet Isaiah:
>> "Here is my servant, whom I have chosen,
>>> My beloved, with whom my soul is well pleased.
>> I will put my Spirit upon him
>>> and he will proclaim justice to the Gentiles.
>> He will not wrangle or cry aloud,
>>> Nor will anyone hear his voice in the streets.
>> He will not break a bruised reed
>>> or quench a smoldering wick

Until he brings justice to victory
And in his name the Gentiles will hope."
(Matt 12:17-21)

Matthew also relates the fourth servant song to Jesus: "He took our infirmities and bore our diseases" (Matt 8:17). Explicit or implicit references to the servant of Isaiah as realized in Jesus are found in many other places in the New Testament, including the Acts of the Apostles and the Pauline letters. There are lingering questions, however, as to whether this identification came from Jesus or from the early church. Some scholars have suggested that it was the apostles and the early community, in light of the resurrection, who made the association between Jesus and the ancient figure in Isaiah.

The strongest evidence, however, is that Jesus himself identified his life and ministry with the suffering servant. There are significant reasons to support this perspective. In the first place, the vast majority of the Jewish leaders anticipated a messiah who would be a brilliant military leader or a charismatic political figure. There is little evidence that anyone expected a messiah who would take on the role of service and suffering. This explains, in part, why the early followers of the Way had to deal with the shock and the scandal of the cross—that the one whom they claimed to be the anointed of God was the same one who was put to death as a criminal in the most brutal form of execution available in the Roman Empire.

Second, Jesus intentionally rejects the titles of messiah, prophet, and king. He consistently refers to himself as *bar enasha*, usually translated as the "Son of Man," but more accurately rendered as the "human being." Jesus is apparently telling us that he is anointed by the Spirit, but not to exercise military or political power. Instead, his life and ministry are intended to model a way of becoming more fully human. In his ministry and manner, in his preaching and practice, Jesus intentionally takes on the role of service and suffering for the sake of healing the human community. Before he is Lord, he is first of all our brother.

FROM SUBSTITUTION TO SOLIDARITY

Our faith tradition affirms that Jesus' suffering, dying, and rising are central to the mystery of our faith. But over the centuries, theologians have given widely differing interpretations for this saving journey. The question is fairly simple. Why did Jesus die? The response is more controversial. Was Jesus sent to suffer and die to appease a God who was angry at sinful humanity? Or did God's love motivate the servant/rabbi from Nazareth to embrace the path of suffering as a way of being in solidarity with all who are marginalized by human injustice? Is Jesus' dying an act of punishment, or a stance of solidarity? Is he making retribution or bringing about healing and restorative justice?

For centuries the dominant perspective on salvation was derived from St. Anselm (eleventh century). It is usually understood as the "satisfaction theory." Anselm, who lived during the time of feudalism, was deeply influenced by the worldview of honor and patronage. In abbreviated form, his approach can be summarized as follows. The sins of humankind offended the honor of God, the sovereign ruler of creation and thereby brought disharmony into the universe. Some form of debt payment was necessary to restore God's honor and to bring back the balance of retributive justice in the universe. Since we human beings owed the debt but could not possibly pay it, Jesus overcame the debt by dying in our place. In this sense, Jesus' death makes "satisfaction" to God for the infinite offense of our sins.

In traditional and later evangelical Protestantism, Anselm's theory gradually developed into the "penal substitution" theory. This approach places a particular emphasis on Romans 6:23 (the wages of sin is death), and sees sinful human beings as subject to God's wrath. The central meaning of the cross, in this perspective, is that Jesus becomes our "substitute," bearing the curse in the place of human beings (Gal 3:13). A large number of Christians, especially in the United States, still accept this penal substitution interpretation as integral to their belief system.

This persistent notion that "somebody has to pay" has its roots in the ancient conviction that human beings have no control over their lives. Their well-being is entirely in the hands of fate, the furies, or the gods. In order to seek protection it is necessary to placate these hidden forces. At one point this practice went as far as sacrificing other human beings—the firstborn, virgins, or other innocent members of the community. Later, the practices evolved away from child sacrifice toward crops or created objects. But the notion of placating or making payment to God still has a strong hold on our religious consciousness.

There are significant signs of change, however. An increasing number of theologians from mainline Christian traditions are challenging the substitution interpretation as a dangerous misunderstanding of the meaning of salvation. They see it as based on a violent interpretation of sacrifice, as well as a misreading of God's fundamental compassion toward creation and human beings. Some are returning to earlier theories of *Christus Victor* that see Jesus' dying and rising as God's final act of liberating human beings by being in solidarity with the suffering and the marginalized. Others, influenced by feminist writers, human rights activists, and liberation theology, are developing contemporary versions of salvation grounded in God's compassion and nonviolent love.

The manner in which we understand the paschal mystery—the dying and rising of Christ and our share in that mystery—has a profound influence on our spirituality and on the way in which we live as disciples of Jesus. There is a critical need to reimage and reclaim the meaning of the cross as God's final and greatest act of solidarity with humanity in Jesus. To stand at the foot of the cross is to see human violence unveiled and ultimately disarmed. The revelation given to us in this scene is that of a God completely without violence, a divine presence in the human Christ that is willing to endure human brutality in order to expose violence for what it is—not the will of God but the desperate measures of frightened and oppressive human perpetrators.[4]

SOLIDARITY AND THE POWER OF NONVIOLENT LOVE

Most people still think of strength in terms of overwhelming physical or military force. Our heroes are more likely to be Rambo or Dirty Harry than Mohandas Gandhi or the women martyrs of El Salvador. This presumption is an understandable but unfortunate outcome of thousands of years of pursuing violence in the name of peace, of practicing retributive justice as a means of restoring some unknown cosmic balance.

What does this say about the transforming power of nonviolence? Is standing side by side in the heat of battle the only kind of solidarity that can make us a "band of brothers"—or sisters? Despite the fact that it has been practiced by some of the most courageous, stalwart people in history, nonviolence is consistently viewed as a sign of weakness. It is widely considered to be the stance of victims, not victors. It may be studied as a curiosity in history, and even held up, at a distance, as the practice of a few idealists. But even at its best, the vision and practice of nonviolence are usually viewed as the tactic of the oppressed. The perpetrators of violence will, of course, encourage their victims to practice nonviolence, and in this case they do indeed mean passivity and surrender. It is understood as the policy of last resort. Or in other words, if you don't have the physical power to overcome, you might look at negotiating for the least painful outcome.

This is capitulation, not nonviolence. Nonviolence arises out of an ethical conviction about the value of life, the dignity of the human person, and the centrality of community. It comes from strength, not weakness, from conviction, not cowardice. It is a chosen stance of life and relationships even before there is any obvious conflict.

9

Embodying the Justice of God

Jesus: The Incarnation of God's Liberating Love

Asian women's theology has been created out of the historical context of Asia's struggle for full humanity. The women of Asia awakened from their long silence and began to speak out of their own language about their experience with the divine.

—Chung Hyun Kyung

There is a direct, intimate relationship between the struggle for social justice and the possibility of experiencing ourselves as loved.

—Roberto S. Goizueta

On the last Sunday of the Christmas season a few years ago, I had the privilege of preaching on Matthew's version of the baptism of Jesus (Matt 3:13-17). In the course of my reflections, I pointed out that the words of radical affirmation that Jesus heard in the depth of his being are also addressed to each of us. To make this more personal, I recall saying something like: "Think of it this way. Through the ongoing journey of your baptism, God is telling you each day: 'You, Margaret, you, Jennifer—you are my beloved daughter. I take great delight in you! And you, Sean, you, Justin—you are my beloved son. I take great delight in you!'"

After the liturgy, as I was standing outside visiting with the parishioners, a young single mother came up to me, carrying her infant son. She smiled and said, "My name is *Jennifer*. When you said my name during Mass, I was stunned. I sat straight up in my pew!" Then her eyes grew large and brimmed with tears. She took a deep breath and went on, "I can certainly picture God saying those words to Jesus. But I cannot imagine God saying them to me."

Jennifer is not alone. We hear countless sermons on love, but many of us quietly wonder if we can ever be lovable. We are taught to believe in God's care for us, but it is difficult to image ourselves as being, in any credible way, "beloved." In a culture of advertising and glib rhetoric, the language and images of love flicker regularly across our television screens. Usually they drift toward the trivial. If passion and love describe every product and consumer promise, it becomes increasingly difficult to know what this means. If love is so diffuse, then trusting that *I am loved* or that *you are loved* is, at the very least, a stretch of the imagination. But the gospel isn't just another talk show or a cultural version of pop psychology. It doesn't tell us that we are necessarily "worthy" of love or that we have a claim on it by reason of personal entitlement. It simply invites us to trust that we are made lovable by the seeking care of God and the affirmation of others who believe in us, no matter what.

LOVE AND JUSTICE

If accepting God's love is a challenge, speaking of divine justice is even more daunting. When most of us think of the justice of God, we spontaneously move toward images of God's *retributive* justice, namely, that the divine judge will eventually, if not in this life certainly in the next, balance out the scales. Good people will finally get the reward they deserve, and the evil will receive their just punishment. To be honest, our concern isn't just about what God will do at the end of our lives or at the end of the world. There is another inner response that I often hear from people and—given my early religious formation—with which I can also readily identify. Call it the "fear of the Lord" or just plain fear mixed with a good measure of guilt, whether real or assumed. To put it bluntly, when many of us hear someone speak of God's justice we begin, figuratively speaking, to expect a lightning bolt followed by a cosmic clap of thunder. We assume that God's justice is primarily concerned about our private moral failings, as though—in our anthropomorphic way of thinking—God has nothing else to do except keep meticulous records of our daily ethical struggles.

Perhaps we can put it another way. Despite all the spiritual rhetoric about love, many of us grow up feeling that we are undeserving of love and unworthy of God's seeking care. In our contemporary culture, I assume that some younger people are growing up with more affirmation (perhaps even a touch of entitlement), but in my generation it was simpler, if not easier, to believe in a God of vengeance than in a God of compassion. For many of us it is more familiar to think of God as being displeased with us than proud of us. It is also more common to visualize justice as facing the consequences of our poor decisions and mistakes than it is to think of God as our advocate and support.

We return then to the foundational question. What *is* the justice of God? What is the shape of divine liberation that is emerging—rising—in the history of salvation and in our human consciousness?

We have explored the ways in which the understanding of justice slowly shifted from a focus on punishment toward a spirit of solidarity with the vulnerable and marginalized. We reviewed the primal images of God as the leader of holy wars against the enemies of Israel, as well as the manner in which these battles reflect the earlier practice of blood avenging in the seminomadic life of the ancient tribes. The exodus event provided the Israelite people with a new experiential model of God's seeking care. In the midst of their exile and slavery, God heard their cries, saw their suffering, knew their pain, and came to deliver them. Because of that dramatic event, a critical change in awareness occurred. Justice began to be understood as God's passionate desire to liberate the oppressed, the divine commitment to stand in fierce solidarity with the poor and the forgotten. This emerging understanding of justice as liberation became the background music for the prophets as they confronted unjust systems in their religious tradition and in the political/economic structures of their time. It is further deepened in the mysterious figure of the servant of the Lord in Isaiah, who hears the call to carry the brokenness of all people toward healing and *shalom*.

This chapter explores the ways in which Jesus experienced God's justice as a transforming power in his life, which in turn compelled him to share that experience with other people. To illustrate this journey, I am focusing on three scenes that reveal Jesus as the embodiment of God's liberating love:

- the baptism of Jesus by John in the Jordan
- the synagogue in Nazareth where Jesus articulates his vision and mission
- the healing of the bent-over woman (Luke 13).

BAPTISM: A TRANSFORMING EXPERIENCE

We cannot understand Jesus' preaching and healing unless we first grasp the depth of his relationship with the mystery of God. Jesus is not in the first place a political leader or a moral teacher, though, as we know, his preaching and ministry clearly challenge the dominant political systems and the legalism of religion. The human Jesus is first of all a disciple centered in God and transformed by that relationship. With the psychological language that is available to us today, we would say that Jesus is a *mystic.*

Despite popular misunderstandings, this does not suggest that he had psychedelic visions, lived in an altered state of consciousness, or levitated off the ground. He is a mystic because he experienced the unconditional love of God at the core of his being. He knew a love that was beyond words, further than human understanding, and past our ability to comprehend. This union with *Abba* ("father") is the sustaining presence, the enduring bond that permeates his life and carries him forward toward his "passing over" (in Luke 9:31, the Greek word is the same as *exodus*) through his suffering and death.

The Gospel of John describes this mystical union in these words: "No one has ever seen God. It is the only Son, who is nearest to the Father's heart, who has made him known" (1:18 [JB]). In this passage, the verb "to make known" is the same Greek word from which we derive the term "exegete"—to reveal, to make more visible, to make radiant, or to interpret. In John's description, Jesus is so united to God that he literally "embodies" that presence in his life and ministry.

How does this experience of divine intimacy manifest itself in the life of Jesus? Obviously, we cannot answer this question with any degree of certainty. We have no way of knowing the inner life of the rabbi from Nazareth. Just as none of us can assume that we fully comprehend our own depths, let alone the spiritual journeys of our sisters and brothers, so it is also impossible for us to describe what unfolded at the core of Jesus' being. But one thing is clear. The Gospel narratives leave little doubt that the baptism of Jesus is a transforming event, a breakthrough to a new awareness of God.

FROM PUNISHMENT TO SOLIDARITY

Jesus comes to the Jordan, where he joins the crowds that are listening attentively to his kinsman, John. This desert prophet speaks of a baptism of repentance in preparation for God's imminent judgment and "the wrath that is to come" (Matt 3:7; Luke 3:7). "Even now," he warns the crowds, "the ax is lying at the root of the trees; every tree therefore that does not bear good fruit is cut down and thrown into the fire" (Matt 3:10; Luke 3:9).

We can recognize in these words the distinctive apocalyptic tone of John's preaching. He champions the coming judgment of God and calls the people to repentance as a personal preparation for the destruction that he believes is imminent:

> I baptize you with water for repentance, but one who is more powerful than I is coming after me: I am not worthy to carry his sandals. He will baptize you with the Holy Spirit and fire. His winnowing fork is in his hand, and he will clear his thresh- ing floor and will gather his wheat into the granary; but the chaff he will burn with unquenchable fire. (Matt 3:11-12)

Some scholars suggest that Matthew may have inserted this pas- sage to reassure the early "followers of the Way" that John's role was only that of a precursor. He is openly declaring that Jesus—not he— is the true Messiah of God. Whatever the case might be, it is John's image of the "coming one" that is our focus here. The Baptist believes that the one-who-is-to-come will be an instrument of God's cleansing wrath, the figure who will "thresh" the world with retributive justice. But, as the Gospel accounts make clear, John's expectation does not come to pass, and when it does not, the Baptist—then in prison under Herod—muses, struggles, and wonders. Given his decisive preaching and his ascetic demeanor, it is doubtful that John's struggle was with his own vision or its consequences. He is portrayed as unmistakably sure of his convictions; more than likely, therefore, his crisis of confi- dence was in relationship to Jesus. He is so puzzled by the direction that Jesus' preaching and ministry had taken that he finally sends his disciples to ask him a direct question: "Are you the one who is to come, or are we to wait for another" (Matt 11:3)? We will return to Jesus' remarkable response later. For now, we need only acknowledge that John's understanding of God's justice and that of Jesus were not the same.

How do they differ? To answer this question we return again to the events unfolding at the Jordan River. Jesus joins the crowds that surround John and waits his turn to experience the baptism of repen- tance. When they come face to face, we have this striking interchange:

John would have prevented him, saying, "I need to be baptized by you, and do you come to me?" But Jesus answered him, "Let it be so now; for it is proper for us in this way to fulfill all righteousness." Then he consented. (Matt 3:14-15)

The term for righteousness (*dikaisoynē*) in this passage is the same word that can be translated as "justice." It is not clear in Matthew's account what form of righteousness Jesus is describing, but in the actual scene of baptism Jesus clearly encounters a form of justice different from that which John was preaching:

And when Jesus had been baptized, just as he came up from the water, suddenly the heavens were opened to him and he saw the Spirit of God descending like a dove and alighting on him. And a voice from heaven said, "This is my Son, the Beloved, with whom I am well pleased." (Matt 3:16-17)

Mark and Luke give differing details of this scene, but all three Synoptic writers agree on the essential nature of Jesus' experience. Jesus came for a baptism of repentance in preparation for God's coming wrath. Instead, he encountered unconditional love—the overwhelming flow of God's presence in solidarity with him. Our translations do not capture the evocative force of Jesus' experience. We might more adequately express it in this way: "You are my Son, the one overflowing with my love [*agapētos*], in whom I take great delight!" The words that Jesus hears echo those of the first servant song in Isaiah:

Here is my servant, whom I uphold,
my chosen, in whom my soul delights;
I have put my spirit upon him;
he will bring forth justice to the nations. (Isa 42:1)

In the baptism of Jesus we witness God's seeking love (*hesed*) converging with God's justice (*tsedaqah*). Love and justice are not opposites. They are not even ultimately in tension with each other. God's seeking initiative, or what is often translated as "loving-kindness" is, in the end, the same as the divine passion to stand at the side of humanity, especially the vulnerable, the lowly, and the little ones.

After Jesus' baptismal encounter, he is immediately "driven by the Spirit" (Mark 1:12) into the desert to be tempted. The recurring phrase used by the tempter to confront and provoke Jesus is directly related to his experience at his baptism: "If you are the Son of God . . . ." The tempter is suggesting the obvious. If you are God's beloved, why not take advantage of it? If you have God's justice on your side, why not use it to make a highly visible political impact? Or, in the taunting words of Herod, in the rock opera *Jesus Christ Superstar,* "Prove to me that you're no fool. Walk across my swimming pool!" There is perhaps no more subtle temptation for any of us than to turn the gift of love into an instrument of ego-driven power.

In the desert temptations, we are faced with another haunting question. How do we know about Jesus' inner struggles? CNN was not there with a satellite hookup to give us eyewitness reporting. According to the Gospel accounts, this was as much a solitary journey into the wasteland of the soul as it was a sojourn into the Transjordanian wilderness. It is, in fact, a classic description of the hero on a vision quest to discover and claim his or her deepest identity. Given Luke's account that after it was over, the tempter "left him for a time" (Luke 4:13), it is likely that these are literary creations brought together in one place to summarize a lifelong struggle for Jesus to choose authentic discipleship. Who of us has not experienced the tug to turn aside and find an easier path? Perhaps at stages along the way Jesus shared these inner struggles with his closest circle of friends and disciples, and they in turn handed the story on to us.

The liberation theologian Juan Mateos describes the temptation scenes as an invitation to abandon the cost of discipleship and instead to embrace the usual forms of cultural success—what he describes as "claiming, controlling and climbing."[1] In more familiar language, we can say that Jesus struggled with the same things that most of us do—with the desire for *possessions, power,* and *prestige.* What Jesus discovered in the desert is similar to what each of us must eventually confront—that being loved is both a gift and a task. In the memorable words of Dietrich Bonhoeffer, there is no such thing as "cheap grace." It is a privilege to encounter the unconditional love of God, but this gift in turn calls us to let go of our ego-centrism in order to confront systems of injustice and to stand by those in need.

GOOD NEWS FOR THE POOR

The baptism is the story of Jesus' inner transformation, of his awareness of being anointed by the Spirit and radically affirmed by God's justice/love. This next scene demonstrates the way in which Jesus comes to value the implications of being God's "beloved." As we will see, Jesus recognized his baptismal encounter with God not as a personal privilege but as a shared mission, a compelling call to proclaim this same liberating justice for all people.

When Jesus learns of John's imprisonment, he first withdraws into solitude and then returns to his roots in Galilee (Luke 4:14-30). When he returns to Nazareth, the local synagogue leader invites him to proclaim the second reading for the Sabbath service and to share his reflections. The synagogue, unlike the Jerusalem temple, was not a place of ritual sacrifice. It was more like a meeting hall—a place of prayer and reflection for the local Jewish community. The usual Sabbath service at this time consisted of the singing of a psalm, the recitation of the *Shema* (Deut 6:4-5), followed by two scripture readings, a sermon on their meaning, and the final priestly blessing from Numbers 6:24-27. The first lesson was from the Pentateuch; the second was from the prophets.

We have no way of knowing if Jewish custom had designated readings, such as we have in our contemporary lectionaries. In any case, Luke gives us an important detail. He notes that "Jesus stood up to read, and the scroll of the prophet Isaiah was given to him. He unrolled the scroll and found the place where it was written . . ." (4:17). In other words, Jesus *intentionally looked for and chose* these words from Isaiah:

> The Spirit of the Lord is upon me,
>   because he has anointed me to bring good news
>   to the poor.
> He has sent me to proclaim liberty to the captives,
>   and recovery of sight to the blind,
>   to let the oppressed go free,
> to proclaim the year of the Lord's favor.
>   (Luke 4:19; cf. Isa 61:1-2)[2]

Jesus sits down. The attention of the whole community is riveted on him. He then delivers what is perhaps the shortest "homily" in history: "Today this scripture has been fulfilled in your hearing" (Luke 4:21).

Luke has given us a remarkable narrative that is both an inaugural vision and a summary of all the themes that are yet to come. Jesus is initially welcomed with praise and adulation, but when the deeper meaning of his preaching becomes evident, he evokes a form of opposition that eventually leads to his passion and death. How can we account for the sudden change of mood in the crowd from admiration to hatred? One explanation is that Luke inserted into this scene the growing opposition to Jesus that came later. This may explain the awkward literary structure of the story, but it does not answer the deeper question. Why did Jesus' message ultimately become a "sign of contradiction," as Simeon had earlier prophesied (Luke 2:34)?

In answering this question, we focus on four aspects of this narrative.

Jesus: Servant of God

First, this story reveals the way in which Jesus understood his identity and his call. Of all the models of religious leadership that were available to him from his Jewish heritage, Jesus explicitly identifies his life with that of the *servant of God* of whom Isaiah spoke long ago. This is a vital clue to the nature of Jesus' self-understanding. As we have seen, the servant was not a military hero in the style of Joshua or a political leader in the tradition of David. He came to bring not a narrow, nationalistic agenda but a universal proclamation of God's solidarity with the poor. In short, the servant was someone who was called to proclaim God's justice/love to *all* the nations, not just to the Jewish people.

Good News for the Poor

The passage also reveals the focus of Jesus' ministry. We come to this narrative already aware that Jesus has been anointed by the Spirit in his baptism. Luke's account outlines in detail the mission that he is given by the same Spirit. Notice that the passage that Jesus chooses is not from the apocalyptic tradition of retributive justice but from the prophets who see God's justice as a liberating presence in history. The emphasis is not on dark threats but on "good news for the poor," not on condemnation but on advocacy for those in need. Jesus, like the servant of Isaiah, is to bring the justice of God—the liberating power of divine solidarity—to those who are economically, physically, and socially marginalized.

The Lord's Year of Favor

Third, by citing Isaiah in this context, Jesus is making an explicit connection between his ministry and the ancient call to a year of Jubilee. As we saw earlier, the Jewish tradition came to understand God's Sabbath not just as a time of rest for the privileged but as a mandate that extends God's compassion and care to all of creation. Every fifty years the fields were to lie fallow that they might be renewed. Refugees and exiles were invited to come home, debts were to be canceled, and the slaves were to be set free. The Greek word for "release" in this passage is *aphesis*. In the Septuagint translation it is the same term that translates the Hebrew word for Jubilee. It is also the word that Luke employs for the forgiveness of sins. Jesus' ministry brings good news to the poor, proclaims *release* to the prisoners, sight for the blind, and freedom for those broken in spirit. This is the call Jesus hears. This is the justice he pursues.

Fulfilled in Your Hearing

Finally, Jesus is telling his community—and all of us—that the ancient call to Jubilee and the vision of Isaiah are no longer far-off dreams or pious suggestions. When he finished the reading, Jesus did not give a long excursus or a lengthy theological explanation. He simply said: "Today, this scripture has been fulfilled in your hearing." *Today. Fulfilled in your hearing.* This is no longer John's imminent judgment—the fiery cleansing that is still to come. Jesus is proclaiming the definitive breakthrough of God's compassion for the poor, the presence of God's solidarity in the "eternal now," that has been unfolding since time began.

FROM BENT OVER TO UPRIGHT: THE HEALING OF A WOMAN ON THE SABBATH

At the synagogue in Nazareth, Jesus asserts his identity and articulates his mission. The rest of the Gospel narratives bring to life what he proclaims in his "inaugural address." There are multiple stories of Jesus' healing presence in the Gospels. I am choosing one that is found only in Luke (13:10-17), not because it is more important but because it illustrates, in a striking manner, Jesus' commitment to justice as liberating love.

The scene opens with Jesus teaching in a synagogue on the Sabbath. A woman is there "with a spirit that had crippled her for eighteen years. She was bent over and was quite unable to stand up straight. When Jesus saw her, he called her over and said, 'Woman, you are set free from your ailment.' When he laid his hands on her, immediately she stood up straight and began praising God" (Luke 13:11-13).

The woman is nameless, as is so often the case in the Gospel stories. For millennia women have been nameless—invisible in their dignity and courage, unrecognized in their leadership, their spirit of solidarity, their commitment to relationships, their creativity, and their faithfulness. She may be nameless, but the fact that she is a woman is all the more significant. Luke is telling us that it is not only physically whole, law-abiding, economically secure Jewish males that can have access to God's favor. Jesus is choosing to widen the circle of compassion, to push out the boundaries of mercy, and to hold up this "daughter of Abraham" (13:16) as a central concern for God's fierce justice.

It is worth noting that Luke describes the woman as living with a "spirit" that had crippled her. Later Jesus is more explicit—he declares that "Satan has held her bound" for all these years. In our contemporary culture we employ medical terms to diagnose illnesses and physical disabilities. In the ancient world many of these conditions were attributed to "evil spirits." They were viewed as a sign that the afflicted persons were "sinners" and were suffering from the consequences of moral failure—either because of their own behaviors or that of their forebears. Thus, this woman would have suffered not only from being crippled physically. She would also have felt the silent disdain, the presumptive moral judgment of the entire community. It wasn't only her body that was bent over; her spirit was crushed and her heart was broken. The fact that she came to the synagogue in the first place is a tribute to her courage.

Jesus, not the woman, initiates the healing encounter. As an observant Jew, the woman would have understood that, given her physical disability, the ritual laws of purity would render Jesus "unclean" if she touched him. She also would have known that asking for healing on the Sabbath would constitute another violation of the Torah. Obviously, Jesus understood this as well, so his decision to heal the woman is a direct confrontation with the religious establishment. We are witnessing not just an act of kindness but a prophetic act of resistance. It is this deeper issue that evokes the wrath of the synagogue official.

The Sabbath, with its multiple rules for observance, was a central religious marker for the Jewish people. In his objection to Jesus' action, the synagogue leader is simply doing his job. He is attempting to enforce the accepted interpretation that healing is a form of work and therefore forbidden on the Sabbath. Jesus' answer confronts this legalism by reconnecting the Sabbath to its original humanitarian concerns. He is reminding them that the "rest" involved on this day is not just about worship or a time of leisure for the privileged. It is also a metaphor for distributive justice—of God's protective care for the well-being of all creatures. Jesus' pointed questions reveal the reasons for his actions:

> Does not each of you on the sabbath untie his ox or his donkey from the manger, and lead it away to give it water? And ought not this woman, a daughter of Abraham whom Satan bound for eighteen long years, be set free from this bondage on the sabbath day?" (13:15-16)

Notice Jesus' use of the words "untie," "release," and "bound." In rabbinic commentaries, there were detailed guidelines indicating which knots could be tied and untied on the Sabbath to care for one's beasts of burden. Jesus seizes this image, challenges its hypocrisy, and then connects it to what he considers to be a far more pressing issue—the knots of physical and emotional oppression that have held this woman "bound" for many years. Even more confining are the legalistic "knots" that fasten her to the stigma of "sinfulness" because of a condition that is beyond her control and certainly beyond her responsibility.

This leads to the second concern, namely, ritual purity. This issue is not directly addressed here, but it is the background music that everyone in the synagogue would have carried in their awareness. The "holiness code," found in Leviticus 17-26, is grounded in this mandate: "Speak to all the congregation of the people of Israel and say to them: You shall be holy, for I the LORD your God am holy" (Lev 19:2). For the faithful Israelite, holiness implied being separated from everything unclean. Purity systems and the laws that surrounded them were common in many cultures in the ancient world. Their purpose, among other things, was to maintain proper social boundaries, to protect the health and well-being of the people, and to promote correct religious observance. In themselves these are understandable, even laudable aims.

However, the laws of ritual purity also had the effect of fragmenting the community by establishing hierarchical divisions. Whatever their original intention, these purity codes created a "social spectrum"—ranging from those who were considered pure and then moving through varying degrees of lesser ritual cleanliness until you reached those who were considered radically impure. Many factors contributed to where one might be on the spectrum of purity, including ethnicity, tribal origin, socioeconomic class, gender, and personal health. In short, the purity laws created a world with "sharp social boundaries: between pure and impure, righteous and unrighteous, whole and not whole, male and female, rich and poor, Jew and Gentile."[3]

When Jesus invites the bent-over woman to approach him, he is walking directly into the jagged margins of prejudice. He is choosing to stand with the exiles and the untouchables. The synagogue leader understood immediately that Jesus was not just a naïve upstart or a do-gooder who had decided, by way of exception, to be kind or considerate. He saw that Jesus was challenging the system itself, calling into question the entire basis of deciding who was righteous and who was not, who was just and who was not.

Jesus does not give us a theological lecture about the meaning of authentic holiness. Instead, he defines it in action. He demonstrates that the most profound way of imitating God's holiness is to stand in solidarity with the poor and the outcast. Compassion is the highest form of holiness. It is not just a personal virtue; it is a sociopolitical stance of justice making. The purity laws divide and exclude. Compassion unites and includes. In Luke's "sermon on the plain," Jesus reshapes the ancient words of Leviticus:

> Be compassionate as your Father is compassionate. Do not judge, and you will not be judged yourselves; do not condemn, and you will not be condemned yourselves; grant pardon, and you will be pardoned. Give, and there will be gifts for you: a full measure, pressed down, shaken together, and running over, will be poured into your lap; because the amount you measure out is the amount you will be given back. (Luke 6:36-38 [JB])

The woman in this story is an icon for each of us. God's liberating justice touches her life and transforms her. She no longer stares at the ground, she gazes at the sky. She is now able to look her sisters and brothers in the eye. She claims her dignity. She is no longer unclean but whole, no longer wounded but well. Through her encounter with Jesus, she has become literally and metaphorically *upright*.

ARE YOU THE ONE?

We return now to the question that John, in prison, sent his disciples to ask Jesus: "Are you the one who is to come, or are we to wait for another" (Matt 11:3)? Jesus responded:

> Go and tell John what you hear and see: the blind receive their sight, the lame walk, the lepers are cleansed, the deaf hear, the dead are raised, and the poor have good news brought to them. And blessed is anyone who takes no offense at me. (Matt 11:4-6)

The response that Jesus gives is instructive. He doesn't tell John's disciples of any messianic ambitions. He doesn't point to a coming catastrophe as a sign of God's judgment upon the world, nor does he paint himself as an exemplar in observing the Torah. He doesn't defend his preaching or his practice of ministry. He simply invites John—and each of us—to listen and to see. Listen with fresh ears, see with new eyes, he tells us. Pay attention to the liberating presence of God at work in your lives and in your world. And join in the same boundary-breaking work of creating community.

10

Proclaiming the Kingdom of God

Jesus as Go'el *for Humanity*

Jesus went throughout Galilee, teaching in their synagogues and proclaiming the good news of the kingdom and curing every disease and every sickness among the people.

—Matthew 4:23

It is no longer possible to kill the voice of justice.

—Archbishop Oscar Romero

At the table of peace will be bread and justice.

—Nedra Ruiz

Before he became the archbishop of San Salvador in 1977, Oscar Romero was considered to be a theological moderate who served the people of his local diocese with quiet dedication. But when he became the spiritual leader of El Salvador, he was suddenly confronted with the enormity of systemic violence that oppressed millions of poor people in his country. Faced with these new realities, he began to speak out with growing determination. Soon his Sunday homilies were being broadcast throughout the countryside. When the right-wing military destroyed the diocesan radio station, a Costa Rican shortwave station began to broadcast his message to all of Central America. On February 24, 1980, he concluded his homily with these words: "I say this in the first person because this week I received a warning that I am on the list of those to be eliminated next week. But let it be known that it is no longer possible to kill the voice of justice."[1]

Exactly a month later, on March 24, 1980, Archbishop Romero was shot to death while celebrating Mass and preaching the gospel of nonviolence.

It is no longer possible to kill the voice of justice. These words reflect both the irony and hope that we encounter in the gospel. The irony speaks of all those who die giving voice to justice. The hope is grounded in the crucified and risen Christ. His transformed, enduring presence in history is both an assurance and a challenge. We are left grappling with questions that can be answered only by following him. If the voice of justice cannot be killed, why do so many women and men who speak it with their lives end up dead? Why do those who seek peace appear to stir up violence? Why do those who work for reconciliation so frequently become a flashpoint for further polarization? Why does the same Jesus who offers us peace as his final gift (John 14:27) tell us earlier that he has come "not for peace, but for division" (Luke 12:51)?

There are no simple answers to these questions. Perhaps that is why the Gospels do not tell us that Jesus is the answer, only that he is the *way*—and that following his way will lead us ultimately to truth and life. But what is this "way"? It is a path of unbending commitment to the voiceless and the forgotten. It is the road that leads him to Jerusalem, a way that he followed as a servant of God's solidarity with the poor, a choice that ultimately cost him his life. Perhaps it would be more correct to say that *Jesus is the question*—the enduring challenge to systems of exclusion and oppression, the voice of justice that will never die. His life of self-giving love, his dedication to the poor, his commitment to nonviolence—even at the cost of his life—are the only answers that God gives us as the path toward peace.

THE DANGEROUS AND SUBVERSIVE MEMORY

Johannes Baptist Metz, a political theologian of the 1980s and 1990s, introduced the prophetic phrase, "the dangerous and subversive memory of Jesus of Nazareth."[2] He was speaking of the way in which Jesus' life, his preaching, his ministry, and eventually his death were experienced as a confrontation with systems of political domination, as well as the cultural and religious institutions that supported and protected them. The early Christians learned, from the beginning, that following Jesus involved a similar confrontation with unjust structures. It meant that they too risked being maligned, rejected, and even eliminated by the "powers that be."

This presents us with an unsettling or, at the very least, a disturbing historical reality. Jesus threatened the structures of injustice in his time, and his early followers found that keeping his memory alive was indeed risky. But the wider screen of Christian history gives us a different story. It tells us of an institution that eventually ceases to confront the structures of oppression and begins—whether for reasons of evangelization or cultural legitimization—to accommodate to the imperial systems of power.

If one reads the classic lives of Christ, there is little that can be considered "dangerous" about his life or memory. For the most part, these authors have portrayed the rabbi from Nazareth in fairly innocuous terms as a moral teacher who preached a generic ethic of caring. Jesus is pictured in pastel shades of kindness. He reaches out to the poor and the marginalized. He heals the sick and comforts the lonely. In this perspective Jesus is viewed through the lenses of personal devotion, as a model of God's love for humankind but separate from the social and political setting in which he preached and lived. This may be an edifying profile of Jesus of Nazareth, but it leaves us with perplexing questions. Why would the Romans execute someone who was merely being kind to others? Why would the religious and political establishment take such offense at his teaching and ministry that they would crucify him?

It is a grave mistake to portray Jesus as one more political revolutionary. His vision, his teaching, and his ministry transcend all political theories and systems. But it is just as fatal to reduce him to a personal savior apart from the radical challenge that his life and teaching offer to structures of injustice. Jesus is not a politician or a military tactician, but his vision has profound political and social implications. He is subversive because he challenges "the brutal normalcy of civilization" in its tendency to promote the powerful and oppress the vulnerable.

THE CRUCIBLE OF THE GOSPEL

Jesus was born into a world of empire. Empire is not only a political matrix for dominative power; it is an entire culture of propaganda, control, and manipulation. Plato writes that the *polis*—the political sphere—is the soul writ large, an outer expression of the inward stance of human consciousness. The political and military instruments that are needed to implement a vision are just that—tools for an institutionalized way of thinking that envisions human beings as objects. It is a system of expediency in which the suppositions are clear, even if they are not articulated. Their rationale includes an assumption that might makes right, that it is necessary to have an upper class and a servant class, and, not least of all, that the purpose of religion in an empire is to preserve and promote what Walter Brueggemann calls "royal consciousness"—the use of religion to legitimize and validate the structures of power.

There were two questions that every young Jewish woman and man faced as they grew up:

- What do we do about the Romans?
- When and how will the reign of God come?

First, there is the "Roman question." What do you do when a foreign empire controls your destiny? At the time of Jesus, the promised inheritance of Abraham, the territory that Moses viewed from a distance, the former kingdom of Solomon and David, was simply an extension of the sprawling Roman Empire. How can you be faithful to your religious vision under a political system that stands in opposition to the most fundamental values in your life?

The Roman garrisons in the towns and villages were the most obvious sign that the Jewish people were a vassal state. But it wasn't just the foreign military presence that was oppressive. The people were also subjected to a worldview that reduced their lives to social expediency. The imperial propaganda proclaimed Caesar as divine and the empire as protector of the people. It boasted of bringing economic and cultural advantages to its citizens, even as it methodically oppressed the very people it claimed to protect. The society was economically and culturally divided into the rich and the poor, the powerful and the powerless, the elite and the masses. Thus, the Jewish population in the first century CE was "occupied" in many ways. Certainly, there was the military, political presence, but behind this was an "occupying rationale"—an overarching cultural and religious claim that the "Divine Augustus" had created the *Pax Romana* with the help and, of course, the approval of the gods.

Second, there is the question of the *basilea tou theou*—the kingdom of God. What will be its nature and makeup? When is it coming? Who will be its leader and what will be the qualities of that leadership?

We can think of the kingdom as God's dream for humanity. Over the millennia the people came to believe that God did indeed have a vision for them. As articulated by the prophets and other wisdom figures, the crux of this vision is that the brokenness and violence of human life will be healed and brought to *shalom*—the peace and shared prosperity of true community. The dream of God is clear: "For surely I know the plans I have for you, says the LORD, plans for your welfare and not for harm, to give you a future with hope" (Jer 29:11). What is not as clear is how this is to be realized. Will it come about by a transformation of human hearts and communities by God's Spirit calling them to work for justice? Or will it be ushered in through violence, either inflicted by God as punishment for the people's sins, or by an army of righteousness fighting evil in the name of God?

Both of these themes are present in the Scriptures. Historically, we have more often argued for violence in pursuing peace than we have claimed the power of nonviolent resistance. Despite the preaching and practice of Jesus and the witness of the early Christian communities, the predominant view has been that peace can be realized only only through some form of justifiable military action.

VARIOUS RESPONSES TO OPPRESSION

How did the various groups among the Jewish people respond to the issue of Roman occupation? And what was their understanding of the coming reign of God? At the risk of oversimplification, we can outline their responses as follows.[3]

Priests and Sadducees

These two groups represented the central religious and political establishment in Jerusalem. The priests were, of course, exclusively male and were held in high regard because they offered ritual sacrifice in the temple on behalf of the rest of Israel. Though the evidence is somewhat sketchy, most scholars have concluded that the Sadducees (from the Hebrew *tsaddiqim*, the "righteous ones") were the central ruling body. They included priests and other political leaders who presided over the Sanhedrin, the supreme ruling council in Jerusalem. It is likely that both the priests and Sadducees would have been educated, wealthy, politically powerful, and strongly influenced by Greco-Roman culture. Given these benefits, it was obviously in their interest to have a comfortable working relationship with Rome. As long as they could maintain the temple and its worship, it was to their advantage to compromise politically and to remain subservient to the empire.

Pharisees

The religious life of Judaism was not limited to the temple or to the priestly caste. The rabbinic tradition, which had arisen in the second century BCE found its primary expression at the time of Jesus in the Pharisees. They were the principal religious leaders for the majority of Jews whose lives were centered in the local synagogues. For various historical and theological reasons, the Pharisees are portrayed in a negative light in the Gospel accounts. In actuality, they were a zealous lay movement that expanded the Jewish spiritual vision beyond the temple for the purpose of keeping the Torah in daily life. The Pharisees' response to the "Roman question" was fairly straightforward: tolerate their political presence but have as little to do with their culture as possible. Though the meaning of the term "Pharisee" is somewhat obscure, most scholars believe that it designates the "separate ones." Thus, their name reflects their religious and political intent. We cannot get the Romans off our backs, they seem to be saying, but we can meticulously obey the Torah as a form of cultural resistance. And obeying the law with exacting zeal may well be the way in which the messianic age will arrive.

Zealots

At the other end of the political spectrum from the priests and Sadducees, we find the Zealots. These were scattered groups of "resistance fighters" who believed that the Jewish establishment in Jerusalem had sold out to the Romans. They also believed that the Pharisees, even with their commitment to cultural and religious separateness, were sacrificing their dignity and freedom for an inauthentic form of survival. The Zealots could harbor no such compromise. They saw no alternative except a violent overthrow of the Roman occupation. The *Sicarii,* or "dagger-men," as the historian Josephus refers to them, were the equivalent of today's terrorists or insurgents.[4] They understood that they would lose in a direct military confrontation with the occupying force, so they used targeted assassinations, disruptions, and mayhem to create widespread fear and intimidation among the occupying forces and their collaborators. For the Zealots, the shape of the coming kingdom was clear; it involved the restoration of the Davidic kingship through a violent revolution.

Essenes

At any time of political and cultural upheaval there are usually individuals and groups who move away from the mainstream population as a way of pursuing religious ideals and protesting against the dominant culture. The Essenes represent such a group. They did not drop out because it was convenient; they did so out of the fierce conviction that most of Jewish society had been corrupted by the occupying enemy. They are likely the sect of Judaism that has been identified with the inhabitants of Qumran and the famous Dead Sea Scrolls, though they also apparently had some small sectarian communities in urban areas. In their monastic-like way of life, they rejected the priesthood in Jerusalem, the leadership of the Sadducees, the religious practices of the Pharisees, and the violence of the Zealots. Like most apocalyptic movements, they believed that society was hopelessly corrupt, and they counted on God to come with purifying power to destroy evil and bring about the messianic age.

JESUS AND THE KINGDOM OF GOD

It doesn't take a leap of imagination to see the groups described above as having parallels in our contemporary world. But where does Jesus fit in this scene? How did he respond to the Roman question? What was his understanding of the reign of God?

In all three of the Synoptic Gospels, Jesus begins his public ministry only after John the Baptist is imprisoned. On hearing this news, *the margins*

Jesus first goes apart and then returns to Galilee and settles in Capernaum by the sea. Galilee is more than a geographical location; it carries immense theological symbolism as well. It was far from the center of Judaism in Jerusalem. It bordered non-Jewish territories and was located on the main caravan routes for the entire Middle East. Consequently, it was a region of mixed nationalities, diverse languages, and a wide spectrum of religious practices. Not surprisingly, it was viewed by the majority of Jews as a place of religious ignorance and ethical contamination. Little wonder that the orthodox Jewish world had long referred to it as the "Galilee of the Gentiles."

But it is precisely here—in a borderland of mixed races and cultures, amid the religiously "impure"—that Jesus locates his ministry. Jesus comes from Galilee, meets his death in Jerusalem, and finally returns to Galilee after his resurrection, where he reveals himself to his apostles, and through their transformed lives to the rest of the world.[5] Jesus proclaims the long-awaited dream of God and then literally "gives it flesh" in his boundary-breaking service to those who live at the borders of life.

In Jesus' preaching and practice, we can identify four distinctive characteristic of the kingdom.

God's Justice Breaking into Human Life

The first of these has to do with God's seeking initiative and overflowing generosity. The kingdom is not of human making; it is a manifestation of God's freedom and gratuitousness. It is not aligned with any particular political movement, nor is it indebted to any military power. It cannot be controlled by legal mandates or explained by religious categories. It is God's unconditional love breaking into human history in a definitive manner.

Just as Jesus had encountered the radical affirmation of "Abba" in his life, so now he proclaims this same divine solidarity as poured out on humanity. This is a kingdom unlike any other in history, before or since. In fact, many commentators today are uncomfortable with the word "kingdom," since it evokes images of imperialism, patriarchy, and oppression. But perhaps that is precisely why Jesus chose this word—to get our attention, to unsettle us with an apparent contradiction, an obvious paradox, a counterintuitive image. Maybe he is speaking and acting with consummate irony. He was, after all, turning the kingdom on its head. He takes the term that the Romans employed for their empire, the language of obeisance to the "divine Caesar," and unilaterally claims it for God's justice instead. The *basilea* that Jesus proclaims and embodies is not oppressive, patriarchal, and excluding. It is empowering, mutual, and inclusive.

The Kingdom Is among You

The second characteristic of the kingdom is that it is already present in our human struggles and brokenness, our pain and our promise. Jesus does not use the language of the Baptist that speaks of an imminent event. He speaks of a mystery that is already at work in the world, already transforming human life. In Mark and Matthew, Jesus announces that the kingdom of God has "come near" (Mark 1:15; Matt 4:17), and he instructs his disciples to tell the people that it has come "very near" (Luke 10:9, 11 [JB]; cf. Matt 10:7). In response to his detractors, Jesus says plainly, "the kingdom of God has come to you" (Matt 12:28; Luke 11:20). Later, when the Pharisees question Jesus about when the kingdom is coming, he gives them this answer:

> The kingdom of God is not coming with things than can be observed; nor will they say "Look, here it is!" or "There it is!" For, in fact, the kingdom of God is among you. (Luke 17:20-21)

In this context, Jesus is illustrating God's love for all creatures, and specifically the fierce solidarity of God's justice with the poor and the outcast. Our task is no longer to wait. Rather, it is to *wake up.* Our call is to become attentive to God's liberating love as it surrounds and envelops our lives. This creative tension between a reality that is already unfolding and not yet fully brought to fulfillment is often referred to by scholars as "realized eschatology." This is a somewhat obtuse way of describing a mysterious unfolding of God's justice/love that is at work now and leading us toward its full realization.

The Kingdom of God Is like . . .

But how are we to recognize this active presence of God in the world? What are its signs? Jesus' response to these questions sets him apart

from John the Baptist and the apocalyptic tradition, which anticipated that the reign of God would come as an astonishing cosmic
event, a mighty battle between good and evil.

This is not the way in which Jesus sees God's in-breaking into
human history. To the surprise—and dismay—of most of his contemporaries, Jesus tells us that the kingdom is already among us, and that
it is manifested in the most ordinary of circumstances. Don't look
first to cosmic catastrophes, Jesus tells us. Look instead to the ebb
and flow of everyday life. In a series of earthy images, Jesus outlines
the vision of God's reign. The kingdom of God, he says, is like a farmer
going out to sow seed; a treasure hidden in a field, a merchant looking for fine pearls, a net cast into the sea, a mustard seed, yeast in a
batch of bread dough, or a woman sweeping her house for a lost coin.
The kingdom is indeed "in our midst." The challenge is to recognize it
in our distractions and preoccupations, in our interruptions and wor-
ries, in the web of our life and relationships, and then to respond to it
by joining God's commitment to justice.

Come to the Feast

The final characteristic of the kingdom is that it is for *all* people. It is
God's passionate desire to stand at the side of every human being—
not just the privileged or the powerful, not only the rich and the
famous, not only the "chosen" and the observant, but *all of the people*.
If anything, there seems to be a preference for those who are ordinarily excluded from the circle of respectability. For most observant Jews
at the time of Jesus, the mobilizing metaphors for the presence of
God were temple and Torah—the ritual cult of sacrifice in Jerusalem
and the rigorous observance of the law in the synagogue.

For Jesus, by way of contrast, it is not temple or Torah that
defines membership in God's reign but the "festive table." It is the
image of God gathering all humanity at the table of abundance that
marks the final breakthrough of love. The signature event in Jesus'
ministry is the meal as an image of the banquet of justice. Jesus ate
with sinners and those who considered themselves sinless; he dined
with Zacchaeus the tax collector and with Simon the Pharisee. His
most frequently mentioned miracle is the multiplication of loaves
(described six times, and included in all four Gospels). The kingdom
of God is imaged, in short, by what contemporary scholars refer to as

"open commensality." This term describes the radical hospitality, the boundary-breaking ministry of Jesus as he shatters ethnic barriers, disregards political borders, crosses the thresholds of strangers, and creates picnics on the hillsides for hungry pilgrims. We cannot understand the deepest meaning of the Last Supper unless we have first grasped the startling inclusivity of these other meals. As Nedra Ruiz reminds us, "At the table of peace will be bread and justice."

The Eucharist is a living reminder that anyone who seeks to be at the table of justice will find a place card with their name on it.

JESUS: *GO'EL* FOR HUMANITY

The dream of God for humanity becomes a living reality in the life and ministry of Jesus of Nazareth. Like many streams flowing into a deep river, his preaching summarizes and carries forward the emerging understanding of justice that had been unfolding for centuries. If God is the *go'el*—the liberator of the people of Israel—then Jesus embodies how far and how deep God's passion to be one with the people will go. Jesus truly is *Emmanuel*—God-with-us. He is *Yeshua*—the liberator of the people. He is also our "kinsman"—our *go'el*—not in the primitive sense of the blood avenger but as the one portrayed in the songs of Isaiah, who gives his blood to heal the people. In Jesus, the justice of God takes on a human face and a compassionate heart. He is God's voice for the voiceless, a hand for the helpless, courage for the fainthearted, compassion for the forgotten. On the other hand, he is a direct challenge to those who are violent, unjust, or oppressive—either in their personal behavior toward others, or because they are colluding, consciously or not, with structures of injustice and domination.

LIVING THE KINGDOM OF GOD TODAY

Exploring the message and praxis of Jesus as a model of doing justice can be hopeful and energizing. But it also carries with it an uncomfortable—even frightening—summons to conversion and action. Responding to this call involves a journey that takes us deeper into discipleship. It plunges us into the swirling current of contradictions that surrounds us daily. It takes us beyond going to church to living the gospel, often at the risk of being ridiculed, dismissed, or even hated.

Our faith tells us that the final outcome of history will vindicate the gospel vision of peace. It will demonstrate that the voice of justice cannot and will not ultimately be killed. But few of us can view human events from the vantage point of divine providence. We do not have the privilege of knowing the final outcome of history. Similar to Jesus and contemporary prophets like Oscar Romero, we must live in the fear and uncertainty of the present.

Several years ago our youth ministry team used the Beatitudes as a discussion tool with the young people who were preparing for confirmation. As part of the exercise, they gave the students a handout to take home and share with their parents regarding our call to work for justice and peace. The next day I received a visit from the father of one of these students. He tossed the handout on my desk and said, "I don't want my kid studying this stuff! It will mess up his mind. You teach him the Ten Commandments and the laws of the Church and that's enough." Instead of listening to the father's concerns, I became defensive and our conversation ended poorly. It was only later, as I reflected back on our interchange that the deeper truth became clear. This concerned parent was correct—in ways that perhaps neither he nor I was aware of in the moment. In this society, taking the Beatitudes seriously can indeed "mess up your mind." They stand in direct contradiction to the values that the media and our dominant culture promote—the values of "claiming, controlling, and climbing." Studying the Beatitudes is part of the "dangerous and subversive memory of Jesus of Nazareth."

The commitment to live a life of justice is demanding to say the least. Jesus struggled with its implications and was tempted, like each of us, to turn aside or to find a more comfortable path. The Gospels offer us several instances of Jesus struggling with his commitment to work for justice:

> I came to bring fire to the earth, and how I wish it were already kindled! I have a baptism with which to be baptized, and what stress I am under until it is completed! Do you think I have come to bring peace to the earth? No, I tell you, but rather division! (Luke 12:49-51)

There are two images in this passage: fire and baptism. In this case, the fire to which Jesus refers is probably not the Holy Spirit or the fiery judgment described earlier by John the Baptist. More likely it is the purifying, challenging force with which Jesus' message will be "cast" upon the earth. As gold and other elements are refined by fire, so will be the structures of society and the lives of individuals by the preaching and praxis of Jesus. His ministry of justice will upset the status quo and bring about divisions and opposition from those who defend the structures of injustice. The second image is that of baptism. Here Jesus is speaking not of the ritual of baptism but of the dark plunging journey—the terrifying ordeal—that he is about to face in his coming suffering, crucifixion, and death.

descent.

Fire and baptism are forceful metaphors. They are mirrored by the compelling, inner emotions with which Jesus describes them. His words convey urgency and passionate commitment, as well as the emotional turmoil that churns inside his life. The word *synechomai* (Luke 12:50), which the NRSV translates as "stressed" is a forceful verb that denotes an actual physical and emotional distress. Jesus confronts his mission with human intensity, and probably profound dread.

To follow in Jesus' footsteps requires a similar kind of passion and commitment. In this section of Luke's Gospel, Jesus is reminding his followers that they must also be prepared for a "baptism"—the cost of following the way of justice. Jesus' language is filled with images of engagement in life: casting out into the deep, burning our own oil, investing our talents in the reign of God, and walking the road to Jerusalem with steadfast hearts. It is not caution or hesitation that is the hallmark of a disciple but courage and the willingness to embrace life's tensions and contradictions. In essence, Jesus is telling us that we cannot be *compassionate*, if we are not first *passionate*—if we do not feel the fire of justice and the power of the Spirit stirring in our hearts.

Inevitably, this stance of engagement will result in conflict, both in our personal relationships and with the dominant culture in which we live. Obviously, there is a need for sensitivity toward the perspectives of others, as well as an attitude of respect in trying to build bridges of understanding. But there is more to being a Christian than keeping the rules or being "nice." The virtue of kindness does not remove the demands of justice. In fact, there are times when compassion calls us to prophetic anger and honest confrontation. Conflict is integral to human growth and community. When approached with honesty and humility, it can serve as a vehicle for authentic communication and can eventually bring about deeper understanding.

11

Living in Solidarity

Paul's Vision of Inclusion

The cup of blessing that we bless, is it not a sharing in the blood of Christ? The bread that we break, is it not a sharing in the body of Christ? Because there is one bread, we who are many are one body, for we all partake of the one bread.

—1 Corinthians 10:16-17

Peace is inextricably linked with equality between women and men.

—U.N. Security Council on Women, Peace, and Security, October 2002

Next to St. Paul's Lutheran Church in La Crosse, Wisconsin, there is a sculpture of the Apostle to the Gentiles. This is not a portrait of Paul the fierce preacher of the gospel. It is not the towering historical figure that dramatically shaped the first generations of Christians. Nor is it the feisty founder of house churches in Thessalonica, Corinth, and Philippi. This is Saul of Tarsus struck down on the road to Damascus. This is the righteous Pharisee brought low by the risen Christ. His mission had been to hunt down the "followers of the Way" and bring them to compliance. But in this portrayal he is the one who is hunted, the pursuer now pursued by God's searchlight. He is blinded, paralyzed, and powerless. And in his helplessness and confusion, in the terrified depths of his being, he hears a question, "Saul, Saul, why do you persecute me?' He asked, 'Who are you, Lord?' The reply came, 'I am Jesus, whom you are persecuting'" (Acts 9:4-5).

This sculpture of Paul is aptly named *Damascus Illumination* since it reflects the blinding presence that became, in turn, a passionate vision of love and justice. I often stopped by this site in the evening after work or on Saturday mornings. I was drawn to this sculpture, perhaps because it reflected the times of confusion and spiritual blindness in my life. It was like looking at a mirror image of myself and standing in prayer before a turning point in Christian history.

There are many ways to be converted, many paths toward finding a renewed vision of God. For some of us, conversion is quiet and inward. Cardinal John Henry Newman described it as coming home to a safe harbor after a long voyage at sea. For others it is an intellectual turning point or an inner form of enlightenment. For Saul of Tarsus it was, if you will, a "head-on collision" with the crucified and risen Christ. It was dramatic, swift, and overwhelming. The scene of Paul's conversion is described three times in the Acts of the Apostles. These accounts were written after Paul's death and decades after his ministry. There is continuing discussion among scholars regarding how much of the Book of Acts is history and how much of it is theological interpretation. Whatever the case may be, the author of Acts clearly sees this event as a turning point in Paul's life and in the history of Christianity.

Who are you, Lord? I am Jesus whom you are persecuting. It is no exaggeration to say that Paul spent the rest of his life trying to understand this question and the startling response that he received. His preaching is nuanced and complex, with rich themes drawn from his expansive intellect, his rabbinic training, and his cosmopolitan background. But beneath these themes is a phrase that occurs again and again in his letters. It is a word image that strives to express his encounter with Christ on the road, an expression that portrays Paul's commitment to the body of Christ as "sacred solidarity." That phrase is *"in Christ."* This expression, which appears more than a hundred times in the authentic letters, captures the meaning of discipleship in the theology of Paul.

Better than any theological excursus, this image describes the profound union that exists between human beings united to God in the risen Christ; and because they are in union with the crucified and risen One, they are also in solidarity with one another. The grain of wheat has fallen onto the ground and died. And a rich harvest is still emerging. The historical Jesus has become the body of Christ in time and space. The consequences of Paul's encounter, his question and the answer that he heard, are still reverberating, like silent waves of grace through our lives and communities of faith.

LORD, WHO ARE YOU?

Paul's encounter with the risen Christ on the Damascus road transformed his life. His theology is not, in the first place, the outcome of a scholarly mind or years of study. It is the result of a life-changing experience that shook him to the core of his being and changed him forever. Unlike Augustine or other theologians, Paul did not arrive at his belief in Christ after a long intellectual journey. He ran headlong into mystery and spent the rest of his life trying to understand the presence that had taken over his life. Paul was aware of being "possessed" by Christ, not as someone whose ability to choose is somehow compromised. It is out of profound freedom that Paul says, "It is no longer I who live, but it is Christ who lives in me" (Gal 2:20). It is with conscious intentionality that he tells us, "You belong to Christ, and Christ belongs to God" (1 Cor 3:23). If the word "experience" has any relevance to the gospel, Paul can claim it in ways that many of us cannot. Although Paul had obviously heard of the "Jesus movement," he had never seen or met what today we call the "historical Jesus." This does not diminish Paul's claim that he had been called personally and directly by the risen Christ. When we read the Apostle to the Gentiles, it is like listening to an impassioned missioner, a fiery pastor, who wants somehow to convey to others what he himself has come to know.

Who was the "Lord" that Paul encountered in the Damascus experience? For the ordinary citizen of the Roman Empire there was only one "Lord"—the "most divine Caesar." The propaganda of the empire and the Greco-Roman culture kept alive the notion that Caesar was a god in human form and that he brought "peace" to the vassal nations who were under the "protection" of his legions.[1] Saul of Tarsus would have been familiar with this rhetoric, since he was a citizen of the Roman Empire and educated in Greco-Roman culture, as well as in the rabbinic theology of Judaism.

Paul's experience of the risen Christ established two unshakable convictions in his mind. The first is that God had raised Jesus from the dead; and, second, if Jesus is raised from the dead, then his ministry of suffering service, his nonviolent confrontation of oppression has been vindicated forever. It is not Caesar or the empire that is Lord, but only Jesus, the crucified and risen Christ. This is the foundational vision of Paul. This is the heart of his "Damascus illumination." The rest of his pastoral and mystical theology flows from this experiential realization.

SOLIDARITY AND EQUALITY IN CHRIST

I am Jesus whom you are persecuting. For Paul this implied not only that Jesus had been raised and vindicated by God, but that those who believe in him share a deep union with him *and* with one another. If the risen Christ is indistinguishable from his followers, then they in turn are united in a new form of community that transcends any form of relationship known in history.

By the time Paul is writing his letters to the communities of Asia Minor in the early 50s, almost two decades have passed since the resurrection of Jesus. We have descriptions of those earlier events in Luke/Acts and the other Gospels, but these accounts were likely not written until the 80s or 90s.

One of the oldest centers for the Jesus movement was the ancient city of Antioch. Ideally situated on the river Orontes, accessible from both land and sea, Antioch was an economic and cultural crossroads for the Greco-Roman world. In this setting the early followers of the Way—probably Greek-speaking converts who had faced persecution in Jerusalem—came to form a community of faith. This community was already flourishing before Saul of Tarsus was converted. Most likely its leaders included women and men, who, long before Acts was written, were forming "prophets and teachers" (Acts 13:1) and sending them forth to preach to the Gentile world.

Through Barnabas and other disciples, Paul became associated with this prophetic group. He was strongly influenced by their vision of Christianity, since it resonated with his inward experience and his emerging convictions. If we were to single out one passage that articulates Paul's vision and its implications, it would be these words from the Letter to the Galatians:

As many of you as were baptized into Christ have clothed yourselves with Christ. There is no longer Jew or Greek, there is no longer slave or free, there is no longer male and female; for all of you are one in Christ Jesus. (Gal 3:27-28)

Many scholars believe that in this passage Paul is quoting an early baptismal profession of faith. Since it emphasizes the egalitarian nature of baptism, it may well have originated in a missionary community like the one found in Antioch and may also have functioned as a "mission statement" for their vision of the gospel. At the very least, it reflects how seriously the earliest Christian disciples took the teaching of Jesus regarding inclusion in the kingdom of God.

Given its cultural context, the communal focus of this passage is remarkable. It acknowledges that baptism is a transforming personal experience, but, just as importantly, it emphasizes the social and political consequences that flow from it. Gentiles are to be welcomed as brothers and sisters; slaves are to be freed; women are called to be in equal partnership with men. Paul is not suggesting that differences have disappeared, but rather that *distinctions*—the oppressive divisions based on ethnicity, socioeconomic class, or gender—have been destroyed by the justice/love of the risen Christ. Galatians 3 gives us an important clue to why the early Christians were seen as a threat to the Roman Empire. It is not only Jesus who is "dangerous and subversive," but anyone who takes his vision seriously and puts it into practice.

No Longer Jew or Greek

In our emerging global cultures, we take for granted that Christianity is open to everyone. What we accept as a given today was not that obvious to those who first heard the gospel. Many of the earliest disciples in Jerusalem believed that God had anointed Jesus as the long-awaited *Jewish* Messiah, that this same God had raised him from the dead, and that Jesus would soon return in glory to destroy the Roman oppressors and bring history to its fulfillment. If this more exclusivist belief had been widely accepted, Christianity may well have been stillborn in Jerusalem. Even after the crucial meeting in Jerusalem (Gal 2:1-10), when the leaders decided to admit Gentile converts without requiring them to be circumcised or to keep the Jewish dietary laws, the conflict was far from settled. As late as the Pastoral letters—near the end of the first century—there were still sectarian factions demanding that Christianity return to a more exclusionary practice. It is sobering to remember that the practice of exclusion—in the form of nationalism, ethnic discrimination, sexism, and racism—has continued to fragment our communities throughout history.

No Longer Slave nor Free

The Roman Empire was organized around strictly hierarchical forms of social relationships. At the top of this class system, under the emperor, were those who belonged to the aristocratic elite, including the senators and the slightly lesser equestrian order. Beneath them were the freeborn lower classes, followed by freedmen and freedwomen, and finally the slaves. Urban slaves were often involved in domestic, educational, and, at times, administrative responsibilities. As a result, unlike their counterparts in the outlying provinces, some of them were able to become rich enough to purchase their freedom. No matter what the conditions, however, slavery was a social condition marked by personal degradation and oppression. Most importantly, slavery was a vital component of imperial economics.

We must keep this sociological background in mind, if we are to understand the threat Christianity initially posed to Greco-Roman culture. This is not just one more religious sect. This is a revolutionary vision of the human person and societal structures. The Oriental cults that flourished throughout the empire also initiated women and men, slave or free, from any ethnic background, as equals. But this was clearly understood as a personal—and private—salvation from the pain and inequity of the world. It had no social or political consequences. This was clearly not the case with the early household churches of Christianity.

Paul's Letter to Philemon gives us a glimpse into this real-life drama. Paul sends the newly baptized slave Onesimus back to Philemon with the expectation that he will be no longer a slave but a beloved brother "both in the flesh and in the Lord" (Philem 16). Clearly, Paul is referring to both the social and political reality of slavery and to the newly won freedom that Onesimus now has in Christ. This is all the more astonishing, given the fact that Paul possessed neither the legal power to set Onesimus free, nor the religious authority to command Philemon to do so. He is appealing to Philemon to welcome back his former slave as "a beloved brother" for two reasons. First, the full, transformative meaning of being "baptized into Christ Jesus" (Rom 6:3), and, second, what we might appropriately call the "presumption

of love"—namely, that Onesimus's former master will, however reluc-
tantly, understand the radical connection between God's liberating
justice and the call to gospel solidarity.[2]

No Longer Male and Female

Finally, to be "clothed in Christ," according to the Galatians mission
statement, also implies confronting the inequality between women
and men. What today we refer to as "sexism" was a socially accepted
reality in the Greco-Roman world. Women were second-class citizens.
This gender bias was built into the civil laws and customs of most
ancient civilizations. The teachings of the philosophers and the sacred
writings of the major world religions simply "blessed" what patriarchy had been practicing for millennia. Early communities like that in
Antioch—and Paul himself—experienced the presence of the risen
Christ in their midst as calling them to a radically different way of
understanding the relationship between women and men.

The declaration of Galatians 3:28 cuts to the heart of patriarchal
privilege.[3] It challenges the proclivity to maintain social stratification
based on dominative power. In effect, it denies all male religious pre-
rogatives in the Christian community based on gender roles. Notice
that Paul is not appealing to a new social philosophy or trying to argue
from political theory. He is simply living out the implications of his
encounter with the crucified and risen Christ. If Jesus is alive and in
union with all who know and follow him, then God's liberating justice
has been vindicated; all structures of inequality and discrimination
have been replaced with a "discipleship of equals."

Perhaps we can understand this startling truth better if we put it
in other terms. Just as someone who was born into Judaism (as in the
case of Paul) had to give up the notion that they alone were the chosen people of God, and just as masters were asked to relinquish their
ownership over slaves, so too husbands were expected to abandon the
power they claimed over their wives. This clearly threatened the status quo in the Greco-Roman world and in traditional Jewish religion.
On the other hand, Paul's vision comes with abundant gifts. This new
relationship "in Christ" celebrates the boundary-breaking energy of
the Spirit that is released into human communities and social structures. It welcomes and affirms the partnership between women and
men. It is the power of Easter transforming the face of the earth.

LATER PAULINE WRITINGS:
TENSIONS AND CONTRADICTIONS

At this point, anyone who has read or studied Paul would ask an obvious question. If this is what Paul articulates as his vision of equality and inclusivity in the early communities, what do we do with the rest of his teaching? The same body of writing that speaks of radical grace, egalitarian communities, partnership ministry, and a vision of inclusion, also seems to endorse, in other places, systems of oppression, including slavery, the subordination of women, and the condemnation of same-gender loving.

How can we explain these apparent tensions in Paul's preaching? For centuries scholars have analyzed the letters of Paul. Though there is still disagreement, most scholars believe that there is a core set of letters that are authentically written by the apostle, while another series of letters are often referred to as "Deutero-Pauline," that is, written in the name and under the authority of Paul by a later author or authors.

In their book *The First Paul: Reclaiming the Radical Visionary behind the Church's Conservative Icon*, Marcus Borg and John Dominic Crossan contend that there are actually "three Pauls" in our Christian writings: the "radical Paul" of the seven genuine letters, the "conservative Paul" of the three disputed letters, and the "reactionary Paul" of what they consider to be the inauthentic letters.[4] Using the latest biblical and historical scholarship, Borg and Crossan argue that the later letters of Paul were actually created by leaders of the early church to dilute the earlier Paul's message and to accommodate it to the dominant Roman culture. Some commentators will no doubt reject this as an extreme interpretation, but I find their reasoning to be sound and I believe their perspective deserves to be taken seriously.

Whether or not they concur with Borg and Crossan, the majority of biblical scholars usually recognize three levels of development in Paul's letters. The earliest stage—what most commentators believe to be "authentic"—reflects the vision of justice and equality of Jesus. The second level—represented by the disputed authorship of Colossians, Ephesians, and Second Thessalonians—reflects a distinct shift away from Paul's earlier writing on equality and justice. These letters seem to be concerned with making the earlier teachings more acceptable in the Greco-Roman culture in which they were being preached. It also appears that these letters are attempting to influence the wider culture by emphasizing the Christian virtues of kindness and respect. But this attempt to dialogue with differing societal values more often than not resulted in the dominant culture moderating and even significantly changing the earlier Christian teaching. An example of this can be found in Colossians 3:22-4:1 and Ephesians 6:5-9, in which slavery is assumed as a normal, acceptable reality, with the proviso that masters treat their slaves fairly and that slaves in turn should "obey your earthly masters with fear and trembling, in singleness of heart, as you obey Christ" (Eph 6:5).

The third and final stage is represented by what the majority of scholars would agree are letters clearly *not* written by Paul—First and Second Timothy, and Titus. The authors of these letters reflect a stance that is no longer trying to influence or engage in dialogue with Greco-Roman society. They have decided simply to accommodate to the patriarchal structures of their time. For example, in the Letter to Titus, we find this harsh command:

> Tell slaves to be submissive to their masters and to give satisfaction in every respect; they are not to talk back, not to pilfer, but to show complete and perfect fidelity, so that in everything they may be an ornament to the doctrine of God our Savior. (2:9)

There is no mention here of mutual obligations, nothing that calls on masters to be respectful toward their slaves. Not only is the institution of slavery taken for granted in this ethical framework, but the onus for making it work is placed directly on the shoulders of the slaves.[5] No matter how one might attempt to justify this perspective, one thing is clear. It is a significant step backwards from the vision of Galatians 3 and the call for radical equality in Christ. We are left wondering what Paul the apostle—the one who encountered the risen Christ on the road to Damascus—would say about all of this.

PAUL'S VISION AND CHURCH HISTORY

What impact did this early accommodation with Greco-Roman culture have on Christianity? Specifically, what effect did this shift toward patriarchal and dominative power have on our vision of biblical justice? From a positive perspective, during the second and third centuries, Christianity became more palatable to the civil leaders in the Roman Empire, resulting eventually in the conversion of the emperor Constantine (313 CE). Obviously, it also lessened the trauma of persecution and made possible the spread of the gospel.

But this early accommodation also came at a price. The Christian leaders' concern to be a stabilizing presence in the empire involved adjusting, if not outrightly compromising significant dimensions of the gospel. Slavery became an accepted part of church life. Women moved away from their earlier leadership roles and, within a few generations, returned to their place as second-class citizens in the community. The practice of radical equality in Christ that Paul had preached became more privatized and focused on the world to come. The forms of leadership in the church began to mirror the Roman political system, or, to put it simply, they became more hierarchical and exclusively male. Under Constantine and Theodosius, Christianity gradually evolved into a *religio*—a civic ethos that reduced belief to cultic worship and gave implicit obeisance to the current political arrangement. Peacemaking became a far-off ideal, as the church found ways of justifying war. Popes became military generals as well as spiritual teachers.

It is not my purpose here to interpret Paul from today's political and cultural context. It is irresponsible to read our contemporary concerns back into Paul's consciousness. Paul is not an early promoter of what we recognize today as democratic government; nor is he an early feminist in the way we understand that term today. Paul's concerns for equality arise out of his encounter with the crucified and risen Christ, not social philosophy. They are rooted in his vision of God as the Father of the human family. For Paul, therefore, the justice of equality "is, first and foremost, about the honor and glory of a just God reflected in a just world. Paul is not thinking primarily about democracy, social justice, or human rights. He is thinking primarily about the honor and glory of God revealed in how Christ lived and died and how the world should live and not die."[6]

RECLAIMING THE VISION OF PAUL

The mission statement of Galatians 3:27-28 may be an ideal, but it is also an ethical mandate. It calls us to reclaim Paul's vision of equality for the human community. Perhaps it was unrealistic to expect the

early Christian movement to reject slavery definitively or to transform the entire social and economic structure of the Roman Empire.
It was probably too much to expect the early church to confront the
Greco-Roman culture with the ongoing practice of equality between
women and men. But does this mean that we give up the challenge of
equality because it was not able to be achieved in the first centuries?
Is it unrealistic to expect that inclusive justice could at least be held
up as a goal inspired by the gospel? Is it merely utopian to expect that
Christianity—once it had achieved stability and social influence—
might use its moral leadership to recover and implement the earlier
teaching of Jesus and the pastoral practice of Paul?

The answers to these questions are understandably difficult and
complex. All the same, we are faced with the sobering reality that the
gospel vision—whether we understand it as an ideal or a command—
has not been consistently pursued, let alone realized. To make matters
more difficult, we have not even fully acknowledged or taken responsibility for the historical events that put the vision "on hold." As the
centuries unfolded, Christian theology gradually overspiritualized
and privatized the social implications of baptism and of the gospel.
By the early Middle Ages the struggle for power between the church
and state had resulted in a standoff or, at best, a working truce. The
church was left with the responsibility of looking after the spiritual
well-being of the people, and, conversely, the state was granted the
power to look after the political, physical concerns of its citizenry.
This division of labor, which is remembered today as the "the cross
and the crown," largely shaped the understanding and practice of justice in the Catholic tradition until the emergence of papal social teaching at the end of the nineteenth century.

There is a curious irony here. The major movements to recognize
the dignity of human persons came not from church leadership but
from grassroots revolutions—often against governments supported
by the power of the church. If anything, church leaders in the eighteenth and nineteenth centuries resisted the populist quest for equality because, in their estimation, it threatened the divinely instituted
order of society. Paul saw slavery as a contradiction to life in Christ,
but it took almost seventeen hundred years of Christian civilization
for the churches finally to condemn slavery as a social institution.
Paul believed that women and men were equal in their baptismal dignity, but it took until 1917 for women to get the right to vote in the
United States—and then only over the objections of many Christian

leaders, or at best with their reluctant support. Only in more recent times have the churches become more visible and supportive of civil rights, women's dignity, alleviation of world hunger, access to health care, arms control, and elimination of global poverty.

But there are also fresh signs of hope. On April 11, 1963, less than two months before he died, Pope John XXIII issued his encyclical *Pacem in Terris,* on the call to work for universal peace. It was his last will and testament, his vision and hope for the human community. Toward the beginning of this work, Angelo Roncalli outlines what he describes as three prophetic signs of the times: (1) concerns for economic justice on behalf of workers throughout the world; (2) the emergence of developing nations and human dignity; and (3) the increasing participation of women in public life. Commenting on the last of these issues, Pope John makes this remarkable statement: "Women are gaining an increasing awareness of their natural dignity. Far from being content with a purely passive role or allowing themselves to be regarded as a kind of instrument, they are demanding both in domestic and in public life the rights and duties which belong to them as human persons" (#41).

Only two years later, at the close of the Second Vatican Council, the Pastoral Constitution on the Church in the Modern World (*Gaudium et Spes*), declared that "with respect to the fundamental rights of the human person, every type of discrimination, whether based on sex, race, color, social condition, language, or religion, is to be overcome and eradicated as contrary to God's intent" (#29).

Even a cursory glance at John XXIII's three prophetic signs of our age challenges us to remember another time and another vision. It summons us back to the "Damascus illumination," an invitation to reclaim the experience of Paul and his vision of radical equality in Christ. The three concerns that are mentioned in *Pacem in Terris*— confronting classism, racism, and sexism—are precisely the same sources of inequality that Paul names in Galatians 3:27-28. Across the millennia, the call to equality is being renewed with fresh energy and commitment. Justice is still rising.

12

Creating the Beloved Community

The Tasks of Justice Today

Those who lead the many to justice shall be like the stars forever.
                                                    —Daniel 12:3 (NAB)

I did not get on the bus to get arrested; I got on the bus to go home . . . I had no idea that history was being made. I was just tired of giving in.
                                                    —Rosa Parks

The ultimate aim of the Southern Christian Leadership Conference is to foster the "beloved community" in America where brotherhood is a reality . . . our ultimate goal is genuine intergroup and interpersonal living integration.
                                                    —Martin Luther King, Jr.

The challenge of working for justice and peace in our time is daunting. If we continue to struggle against systems of oppression, we will inevitably face challenges that are difficult, demanding, and at times downright disheartening. In these moments, the choices open to us often appear unproductive and self-defeating. Either we give up altogether and withdraw into a private world of survival, hoping that the chaos will go away, or we opt for vague generalities and utopian slogans without staying engaged in the ongoing struggle. It is difficult to walk the uncertain ground between these two options, namely, staying engaged in the work of reform without reducing it to pious sentiments. Is it possible to be both hopeful *and* realistic? Can we remain committed for the long haul and not give up when we do not see results?

As a way of addressing these questions, I invite the reader to reflect on two persons from our recent past who creatively carried this tension between courage and fear, hope and realism. It is not my intention to place them on a pedestal. Actually it is quite the opposite. I want to describe them in terms that are realistic and accessible. In their willingness to take personal risks when the circumstances of history summoned them, they became profiles of "those who lead the many to justice" (Dan 12:3).

ROSA PARKS AND MARTIN LUTHER KING, JR.: CONVICTION AND COMPASSION

The civil rights movement in the United States began in earnest when history hurled two people into the maelstrom of injustice and summoned them to a prophetic response.

First there is Rosa Parks. On December 1, 1955, after a long day's work as a department store seamstress, bone-weary and physically in pain, Rosa boarded a city bus in Montgomery, Alabama, to go home. She paid her fare and took a seat in the "colored" section. As the bus filled up, the driver demanded that she move to the back of the bus, so a white man could sit down. She refused and was arrested. Later, Rosa said that she was not only physically weary, she was, most of all, "tired of giving in." She was tired of being oppressed, weary of being exploited, fed up with being sent to the back seat of life because of her race. When Rosa Parks chose to remain seated she in effect stood up for herself. She also stood up for the human dignity and equality of all people, especially those pushed to the margins. In that simple, reflective choice, she unknowingly became the "mother of the civil rights movement."

Often the most courageous acts occur quietly and far from public notice. But in this case, a woman's silent courage, on a city bus at rush hour, set in motion a chain of events that literally changed history. Her arrest and subsequent night in jail became the event that galvanized the black community in Montgomery and set in motion the famed bus boycott that caused the segregation laws first to falter and then finally to collapse.

The second person in this drama is the Rev. Martin Luther King, Jr. At the time, he was completing his doctorate in systematic theology at Boston University and had just begun serving his first pastorate at the Dexter Street Baptist Church, also in Montgomery. Like Ms. Parks, he did not come to his assignment with a preconceived plan. His training had prepared him for ministry, but it was not foremost in his mind—or marked on his calendar—to confront the racism of white America. One of his early sermons was on the three dimensions of becoming a mature Christian; certainly a spiritually relevant topic, but not exactly unsettling to the structures of the dominant culture.

When Rosa Parks sat down, Martin Luther King was challenged to stand up. And stand up he did. He accepted the leadership of this historic nonviolent action to confront the laws of segregation in the United States. What Rosa began with her act of courage, Martin sustained with his theological vision and preaching. The boycott lasted 382 days. On December 21, 1956, the Supreme Court declared unconstitutional the existing Jim Crow laws of segregation. During these months, King was arrested, his home was bombed, and he was subjected to personal abuse. But his real work had just begun.

Modeling Lives of Justice Making

We look to Rosa Parks and Martin Luther King, Jr., not because they are famous but because they are *human beings*, ordinary people who worked, loved, dreamed, and struggled like the rest of us. They are not the only persons who, in the midst of their busy lives, encounter a turning point and choose to act with courage in the face of injustice. There are millions of people who make similar decisions every day that take them beyond personal safety into the world of service, beyond self-preoccupation to altruism. It is precisely because Rosa and Martin are profiles of practicality—putting their convictions into action—that they call us to a similar path. They are celebrated public figures who worked for justice, but their attitudes and actions are reflected in other unheralded people each day. There are four ways in which their challenges and choices invite us to follow a similar path.

Choosing to Act

First, they *chose to act* when faced with injustice; they didn't just look the other way. They didn't step back in fear when the pain of their sisters and brothers summoned them to respond with courage. There is a widespread misunderstanding that courageous people are individuals who do not know fear. This is simply not the case. Fear is an integral dimension of being human. It is the psychic energy of protection, the body's alarm system in the face of danger. One of the most frequent affirmations in the Scriptures is "Do not be afraid." Perhaps we are given this encouragement precisely because each of us faces and carries fear so often. Courageous people are not beyond fear; they simply choose not to act out of their fear. They are not "fused" with their fear; they are not "frozen" in dread or paralyzed by anxiety. They reach toward another depth. They move beneath the fear to claim the convictions that shape their lives—to the image of the creator at the center of their being. It is from this quiet intensity that they choose to respond. We live in a world of fear, but each of us can choose to transcend our timidity and to engage in the demanding work of justice.

Commitment to Community

Second, both Rosa Parks and Martin Luther King, Jr., were *engaged in life and community*. On a personal level, they were living reflective, intentional lives, but in addition—long before the actions that made them public figures—they were already involved in communities that were committed to the work of justice. At the time of the Montgomery bus boycott, there was a popular assumption that Rosa Parks was simply a quiet, reserved woman who was physically weary the day she got arrested, and that happenstance became the flashpoint of a great movement. Rosa was indeed tired, but she was not a passive observer who accidentally came down on the wrong side of the law. In addition to being active in her church, Rosa was also involved in grassroots organizations that promoted equality for African American citizens.

A Faith That Does Justice

Third, their response to injustice grew out of their *religious faith and convictions*. This is an important element in their lives and ours, because it signals a reenergized understanding of the role of faith in public life. Frequently, the message of the churches has been that religion and politics don't mix. Religion, in this perspective, is about saving our eternal souls, about getting to heaven; it is otherworldly, private, and apart from the structures of political life. If anything, religion and the Bible were often used—incorrectly and inappropriately—to support and defend unjust political structures.

Gradually this began to change. During the movement toward woman's suffrage, many of the female leaders were theologically well educated. They turned to the prophetic tradition and its call to authentic justice to confront the manipulative manner in which Scripture had been used to reinforce patriarchy. The Scriptures had also been employed for centuries to justify slavery. It was only during the abolitionist movement that a different, more authentic reading of the word of God began to emerge. The civil war might have ended slavery, but it did not halt prejudice or de facto discrimination in the form of segregation. "Separate but equal" more often than not meant separate and marginalized. With the Montgomery boycott the Christian churches became more actively involved. The dignity of the human person, economic justice, and poverty moved from the periphery of religion to the foreground. Ministers, priests, rabbis, nuns, and other women and men of faith, often at great personal cost and suffering, marched in the streets, grounding their actions on the biblical mandate to fight injustice. Rosa Parks gave this movement a face. Martin Luther King gave it a theological vision and a prophet's voice.

Becoming a Long-Distance Disciple

Fourth, both Rosa Parks and Martin Luther King, Jr., continued to *evolve and grow* as they negotiated the treacherous waters of prejudice and hatred. Rosa Parks grew up in the same Southern culture where her grandfather had been a slave. She recognized the face of discrimination and the bleak world of segregated living. As a child she attended a Quaker school and found there a setting in which her innate gifts were formed and flourished. She may have been shy and self-effacing, but she was also confident and sure of her convictions.

She and her husband, Raymond, were both active in the civil rights movement before it became popular. They were involved in voter registration drives for African Americans, and Rosa was the secretary for the Montgomery branch of the NAACP. In her role as youth director for that organization, she was preparing for a major youth conference when she was arrested for not giving up her seat on the bus. Following that historic day in Montgomery, Ms. Parks continued her work with the civil rights movement, receiving several citations, awards, and honorary degrees before her death in 2005.

Rosa Parks was a long-distance disciple, a woman who lived out of her convictions and continued to grow in the face of immense challenges. She was a woman of justice in her heart before she became a prophet of justice in the streets of Alabama. Her decision on that fateful December afternoon did not come out of passivity, desperation, or being physically weary. It came from a reservoir of values and a long history of spiritual reflection.

TOWARD THE BELOVED COMMUNITY

The commitment to grow in discipleship is evident also in the life and ministry of Dr. King. He came from a family legacy of ministers and public servants. In the seminary, among other philosophers and theologians he studied, he was deeply influenced by Mohandas Gandhi's vision of *satyagraha* (soul-force), as well as his practice of nonviolent resistance in India's struggle against British colonialism in the 1930s. In his writings, sermons, and speeches, we hear echoes of the Hebrew prophets and the Christian gospel. He is formed in the ancient passion of justice for the poor, along with the central notion of *agapē*— the generous love of God revealed in Jesus. If Jesus was Martin Luther King's motivating vision, Mohandas Gandhi, in turn, gave him a practical method to live it in the spirit of nonviolence.

In the early stages of the civil rights movement the focus was on overcoming the unjust laws of segregation and realizing the long-delayed human rights of African Americans in the United States. But as the work progressed it became clear to Dr. King that this was about much more than confronting racial injustice; it was also about deepening the bonds between all races by helping them to understand their common dignity in God. Integration, as King understood it, is more inclusive and far more demanding than desegregation. The latter might be able to eliminate discrimination in housing, employment, education, and public accommodations by the passage of laws. But the wider goal of integration cannot come about by legislation or judicial mandate. It requires a transformation of hearts and attitudes, the long and arduous journey to understand that, underneath all our differences, we are one human community.

After he won the Nobel Peace Prize in 1966, Martin Luther King, Jr., expanded his work to the North. His developing vision included confronting other issues that contributed to global injustice, including poverty, corporate greed, economic injustice, structural violence, and militarism. This expansion of his ministry reinforced and deepened a theme that King had spoken and written about from the beginning of his ministry, namely, the image of "the beloved community."

The idea for a "beloved community" developed long before King gave it renewed energy in the 1950s and 1960s. Late-nineteenth- and twentieth-century thinkers such Walter Rauschenbusch, Josiah Royce, and Reinhold Niebuhr had combined Christian teaching on justice with the practice of moral compassion to describe their emerging ideal of a healed and reconciled humanity. Ultimately, this image is a contemporary version of what Jesus practiced in his teaching regarding the kingdom of God. Dr. King believed that the beloved community could be achieved only through the power of redemptive suffering, especially as it is embodied in Jesus' ministry and his confrontation with injustice. The beloved community is, therefore, far more than a utopian dream. On the contrary, it is essentially the same as choosing to walk the road to Jerusalem and to Calvary. It will come about only if there are people who, like Jesus, are willing to put their values into action, disciples who are willing to give their lives to transform the violence of society.

In March of 1966 Dr. King led the March to Montgomery. After it was over, several thousand of the participants were delayed at the airport because of weather. King later recalled how moved he was to witness this diversity and solidarity in the human community. "As I stood with them and saw white and Negro, nuns and priests, ministers and rabbis, labor organizers, lawyers, doctors, housemaids and shop workers brimming with vitality and enjoying a rare comradeship, I knew I was seeing a microcosm of the mankind of the future in this moment of luminous and genuine brotherhood."[1]

There are three underlying spiritual principles at work in the image of the beloved community. The first is that human beings are created for relationships; we are not designed by God to be economic or spiritual lone rangers. Second, community is difficult and spiritually costly, because it will demand that altruism be greater than selfishness, that generosity become more expansive than greed, and that compassion be stronger than competition. Third, there is a need for personal and communal conversion, a long-term commitment to compassion as a way of life.

Dr. King recognized that creating the beloved community is a task that cannot be realized in one person's lifetime, or even perhaps in the course of human history. This is ultimately an endeavor that goes beyond human effort. He spoke often of avoiding what he called "a superficial optimism," on the one hand, and "a crippling pessimism," on the other. He understood that the solutions to injustice involve a slow process, a long pilgrimage toward a promised land that we may never fully enter. At one point, he put this vision in these words:

> Although man's moral pilgrimage may never reach a destination point on earth, his never-ceasing strivings may bring him ever closer to the city of righteousness. And though the Kingdom of God may remain not yet a universal reality in history . . . we must be reminded anew that God is at work in his universe. He is not outside the world looking on with a sort of cold indifference. . . . As we struggle to defeat the forces of evil, the God of the universe struggles with us. Evil dies on the seashore, not merely because of man's endless struggle against it, but because of God's power to defeat it.[2]

BECOMING THE BELOVED COMMUNITY

In recent decades there has been an ongoing discussion regarding the difference between the works of charity and the responsibilities of justice. Those who disapprove of religious activists being involved in working for justice and peace often point to the fact that Jesus said that his kingdom is not of this world, and that we should not mix politics and faith. For them, the church's role is to provide charity to those in crisis, but not necessarily to confront the systems of injustice that create these conditions. On the other hand, many of those who have been involved in working for civil rights, participating in the peace movement, and confronting the structures of violence have been critical of the institutional church for a one-sided emphasis on charity at the expense of neglecting issues of justice.

I recall a conversation that I had several years ago with a prison chaplain. At the corrections facility where he served, there had been years of abuse, neglect, and violence toward the inmates that finally resulted in a prison riot during a bitterly cold winter night. In addition to widespread destruction and injuries, several prisoners died from the subzero temperatures when they were forcibly evacuated to the prison yard for the remainder of the night. The local churches responded by giving food, money, and blankets to the surviving inmates, but no one raised the question of institutional violence. The prison chaplain's response was instructive and quietly prophetic. "The churches mean well," he told me, "and we are grateful for their help, but they only seem willing to help the victims. They are not willing to confront the system that victimizes them."

Perhaps, over the centuries, we have created a false dichotomy. We do not have to choose between the works of charity and the tasks of justice, since we are summoned to do both. We can provide blankets *and* raise our voices against unjust structures. We can, to echo the words of Archbishop Dom Helder Camara, feed the hungry *and* confront systems that create hunger and poverty. In his encyclical *Caritas in Veritate* (*Charity in Truth*), Pope Benedict XVI asserts that charity is the heart of Catholic social teaching: "Love—*caritas*—is an extraordinary force which leads people to opt for courageous and generous engagement in the field of justice and peace" (#1).[3]

Creating human community is not a project that we can develop or a goal that we can accomplish on our own. It is a gift that God has already given us in the crucified and risen Christ. We do not need to save the world, or to build the kingdom, or to create the beloved community. God has already initiated this work in creation and in the history of salvation. But this does not lesson our responsibility, since God's offer of healed relationships also requires that we embrace and live the gift that has been freely given. In the Christian Scriptures the Greek word for community is *koinōnia*. The Protestant tradition usually translates this as "fellowship," whereas Catholics often prefer the term "communion" or simply community. In whatever manner we translate it, *koinōnia* is not a dream that we can realize by human effort alone. It is God's healing gift of relationships brought about in Christ. It is also a task that each of us carries quietly in our daily lives.

It is also an invitation to appreciate more deeply the earthy, humble metaphors that Jesus uses to describe the kingdom of God at work in our lives: a mustard seed, a small amount of leaven, a treasure hidden in a field, grains of wheat thrown into the wind, shepherds, fishermen, women, children, and the vulnerable in our midst. There is little evidence here of forces that are politically powerful or socially influential; only the quiet, apparently insignificant work of grace unfolding in ordinary peoples' lives.

This quiet, persistent growth is the way in which we help "realize" the justice of God in our circle of relationships. Our task is not to save the world but to demonstrate in our lives that we seek to be free from hatred and committed to equality. Our task is to make the kingdom of God—the unconditional love of God breaking into the world—more visible and alive in our lives and relationships.

Rather than describe this in the abstract, the following is a word portrait of people that I consider to be examples of "justice workers." The reader can easily expand on these examples from his or her own circle of relationships:

- A couple who cared for their son with muscular dystrophy with loving devotion until he died in his early thirties, and who continue to serve as health care workers and lay ecclesial ministers in their parish community.
- A woman in her early sixties, living with multiple sclerosis, who, with the support of her husband, reaches out regularly to immigrant families in need of advocacy and support.
- A gifted entertainer who created time in between engagements to care for his elderly parents in their final years, offering them love, support, and home-cooked meals.
- An editor and publisher who, with imagination and creativity, continues his career by working from his home, so that he can personally care for his wife of many years as she lives with Alzheimer's.
- Members of women's religious congregations throughout the world who continue to educate, serve the poor, care for the sick, and confront systems of injustice, even as they are questioned by church authorities regarding their orthodoxy and loyalty.
- A nurse practitioner who uses her specialized skills in cardiology to serve the medical needs of veterans and their families, even when she has to work longer hours with no additional pay.
- A retired teacher who, with the support and help of her husband, dedicates her time and energy to providing home health care to the elderly and others whose health is failing.
- A young woman who completed her master of divinity degree and feels called to ordination in the Catholic Church; but since

that is not allowed, she is giving her life in service to empower
poor and vulnerable women and children.

- A gifted woman in her forties who directs a nonprofit organization with passion and generosity. After surviving painful relationships in her family, she reaches out in compassion and care
to others.
- The dedicated women and men who serve in Catholic Worker
houses, L'Arche communities, homeless shelters, free clinics,
refuge houses for women victims of domestic violence, St. Vin-
cent de Paul centers, parish nurse programs, prison ministry,
and other ministries of care.
- The growing number of courageous people—lay, religious, seekers, and nonbelievers—who are working to overcome international sex trafficking by creating safe transitional housing,
counseling, and education for women and children who have
been sold into slavery.
- A Native American pastoral leader, with a master's degree in
theology, who has helped develop a program of advocacy and
outreach for victim/survivors of clergy sexual malpractice.
- A single woman who, in her work as a postal employee, advocates for the poor, collects food, and works for greater community involvement in issues of justice.

It is precisely here—in schools, homes, offices, stores, TV stations,
hospitals, farms, malls, hotels, fishing boats, restaurants, airports,
nursing homes, loading docks, bus stations, food pantries, homeless
shelters, and health clinics—that we see signs of hope. In the midst of
a world of escalating violence and fragmented relationships, ordinary
people are quietly transforming our world. This movement is being led
by people who do not expect recognition, do not seek awards, and do
not expect to be applauded in the media. They are simply performing
the "small acts of courage" that Rosa Parks, Martin Luther King, Jr.,
and many other activists have taken on in their lives. This commitment to create bonds of reconciliation and healing is largely unseen
and unnoticed. But it is a reminder, as Georges Bernanos writes, that
"grace is everywhere."

13

Moving beyond Armageddon

The Call to Responsibility and Solidarity

As he came near and saw the city, he wept over it, saying, "If you, even you, had only recognized on this day the things that make for peace! But now they are hidden from your eyes."
—Luke 19:41-42

I know there are lots of wars, environmental problems, and people suffering from poverty and disease. But I don't have to worry about all that, because I'm going to be raptured before things get too bad.
—Born-again college student

THE THINGS THAT MAKE FOR PEACE

On the eve of his passion and dying, as Jesus was about to enter Jerusalem, he paused at the crest of the Mount of Olives to gaze at the revered city of his people. Luke tells us simply that Jesus "wept over it." He is in a long tradition of prophets who experienced profound sorrow on behalf of their people and their future (see, e.g., Jer 9:1; 13:7; Neh 1:4).

If you, even you, had only recognized. . . . In our families and relationships, in our times of personal crisis or brokenness, we might not use these exact words, but we are acquainted with a similar ache in our hearts. In reading the newspaper, or watching the evening news, or checking Internet updates, we might not describe our emotions in the same way, but if we are honest, we might identify with a similar depth of loss. Jesus wept because of the blindness of the religious leaders and the lack of awareness among the people. But he also wept because he anticipated what was to unfold in a few decades when the Romans, under the leadership of Titus, would lay siege to Jerusalem and destroy the temple:

> Indeed, the days will come upon you, when your enemies will set up ramparts around you and surround you, and hem you in on every side. They will crush you to the ground, you and your children within you, and they will not leave within you one stone upon another; because you did not recognize the time of your visitation from God. (Luke 19:43-44)

What are the things that make for peace? We live almost two thousand years after this scene on the Mount of Olives, but we have not drawn much closer to the practice of justice or the realization of *shalom* in the human community. The answers given today are as varied and contradictory as they were when Jesus, the *bar enasha* (the "human being"), processed into Jerusalem. He rode into his city on a donkey, a beast of burden, a presence of peace—and the anti-symbol of political and military power.

After the death and resurrection of Jesus, his followers were challenged to revise their understanding of messianic expectations, political power, and the direction of history. From every indication, the first disciples, including Paul and the early household churches, expected Jesus to return soon—for many of them, in their own lifetime. When this did not occur, it did not change the core message of the gospel, but it did transform the horizons of our hope. The kingdom of God is emerging, even if it is quiet and hidden like a mustard seed that falls into the earth or a bit of leaven thrown into the immense batch of history. Time, it seems, has always been running out. The question of when the final realization of the kingdom would come and what it would look like has only grown in our consciousness—in our anxiety and anticipation—over the centuries. Today it has become an obsessive focus of interest and speculation.

THE END IS ALWAYS NEAR

I was not aware, as I was growing up, that the earth has an expiration date. A lively debate is unfolding in the scientific community regarding the possibility of what some describe as the "Big Crunch"—the cosmic reverse of the "Big Bang" some 13.7 billion years ago. As the expanding universe reaches its outer limits, this theory maintains, it will likely turn back on itself and begin a regressive journey toward extinction. Since this possibility, according to the best estimates, is still billions of years away, it remains more in the category of a fascinating hypothesis.

But scientists and the human community are facing a more immediate crisis. Environmental experts and advocates are gravely concerned about the climate changes that are endangering our planet and its bioregions. More life forms are headed for extinction each year, and the list of endangered species keeps growing. The human carbon footprint is beginning to surpass the earth's built-in regenerative power. We are beyond urgency. We are rapidly approaching a global crisis.

Unfortunately, these real emergencies are often trumped by psychic denial, resistance to change, fear of the future, or the adamant refusal to take responsibility for the present. The urgency surrounding the environment, wars, poverty, and our dwindling resources is not attracting the level of popular attention that other, more fascinating end-of-the-world scenarios do. As I am writing, the popular media, New Age enthusiasts, and many fundamentalist Christian groups are pointing to 2012 as the coming end of the world. According to these theories, the ancient Mayan calendar has scheduled it, the Chinese sages wrote about it, and the Book of Revelation has foretold it.

Looking back at human history it appears that the end has always been near. Over the centuries there have been thousands of individuals who claimed to have privileged information regarding the exact time when the world would end. So far, since we are still here to comment on it, they have apparently been incorrect. But that hasn't prevented us from being interested in—even obsessed by—these future predictions of our demise.

A Portuguese proverb reminds us that "as soon as you are born, you are old enough to die." Our lives, whether measured in days, months, or decades, are tiny droplets in the vast ocean of time. This awareness of human mortality is central to our angst as finite creatures. It is related not only to the inevitability of death but also to the daily experiences of loss. Beneath our bravado, we struggle with the fear of losing our loved ones, our dreams, our health, our status, and our security. Without realizing it, this fear of loss can become a subconscious force driving us toward greed, the abuse of power, interpersonal violence, and, eventually, even war.

As reflective self-consciousness emerged in time and space, it was unavoidable that human beings would contemplate not only their own personal death but the end of time itself. So, we might rephrase the proverb: as soon as the human community became aware of history, it began to worry about the limits of time. More to the point, it eventually began to *predict* its demise—to give dates and times for the end of our cosmic journey.

In theological terms we describe this limit point in time as "eschatology"—from the Greek word *eschaton*, meaning that which is "last" or "farthest." Eschatology reflects on the final goal or consummation of human history. When is the world going to end? The answer to this question is related to how we view the tasks of justice and peace in our human community. It is likewise grounded in our understanding of God. Finally, it depends on the way in which we regard the unity of the human race and whether we consider ourselves to be members of the "elect" or not.

We can safely assume that every human being and every believing person wants peace. Similarly, we can presume that everyone believes in the need for justice. The difficulties arise in how individuals and religious communities understand justice and peace, and even more urgently, what means we are to pursue to achieve our dreams. Will peace come about by a military victory over our enemies? Or will it be realized through the demanding work of establishing a more just world? If we choose the first option, then religion must be enlisted as part of the ideology that supports the wars that will eventually lead to peace. If we choose the second option, the primary task of religious institutions is to create the vision and practice of restorative justice as the condition of the possibility of peace.

ARMAGEDDON AND APOCALYPSE: A FUNDAMENTALIST CHRISTIAN VIEW

Since the tragic events of September 11, 2001, human anxiety has continued to escalate. The world is focused on terrorism as a movement that threatens our dreams and civilization itself. Here we face another sad reality. It is not just that terrorism is thriving. It is doing so as an expression of *religious* conviction. Religion is no longer primarily a power for healing and unity; it has become a tool for social division and violence. It would be a grave mistake, however, to identify this religious fanaticism as coming only from the world of Islam. There is increasing evidence of a fundamentalist wing in most world religions that advocates some form of violence in the name of religious values. Sadly, this is also true of some adherents of Christianity.

According to many estimates there are about twenty-five million fundamentalist Christians in the United States. They may be in the minority compared to other mainstream Christian denominations, but the impact of their beliefs regarding the end-time has had a wider impact on our culture than their numerical presence would suggest. Their predictions about the manner and timing of the coming catastrophe have not only shaped the response of ordinary people but also influenced our approach to international relations and even our foreign policy. Throughout the centuries, there have been individuals who predicted the end of the world, but the particular version that is most widespread among fundamentalist Christians is relatively recent.

It is usually referred to as "premillennial dispensationalism," based on the belief that God has divided history into distinct ages or "dispensations." This teaching emerged in nineteenth-century England and was brought to the United States by John Nelson Darby, a missionary who preached this doctrine at evangelical gatherings. Most mainline Christian denominations believe that there will be a second coming of Jesus at a time and in a manner beyond our knowledge and understanding. Darby's preaching—and that of his contemporary proponents—differs significantly from this view. Basing their convictions on a literal, uncritical reading of selected passages from the Bible, they believe that there will be a two-stage return of Christ.

In abbreviated form, this end-time scenario includes the following events. First, there must be the rebirth of the nation of Israel, followed by the "rapture" of born-again Christians into the heavens. The rest of humanity will then face God's wrath in a series of plagues, wars, and other global catastrophes. This time of tribulation will also include the appearance of the Antichrist, the rebuilding of the temple in Jerusalem, and its subsequent desecration. All of these events will result in the great battle of Armageddon, led by the returning, glorious, warrior Christ. After his decisive victory, Jesus will establish his millennial kingdom on the throne of David in Jerusalem. Finally, after reigning for a thousand years, the last judgment will occur and eternity will begin.

Admittedly, this is an oversimplified version of a rather complex set of predictions. This core explanation was given wide publicity and popular credence because of books like Hal Lindsey's *The Late Great Planet Earth*, which he co-authored in 1970 and which has sold millions of copies worldwide.[1] Lindsey originally predicted that the end of the world would come about in the next generation, or in other words sometime in the late 1980s. In subsequent books and in his current work, he has adjusted the timing to fit the unfolding of contemporary world events.

This doomsday approach to contemporary history has received a new surge of publicity and popularity through the novels in the Left Behind series by Tim LaHaye and Jerry Jenkins. These fictional accounts are a blend of fast-paced violence, natural catastrophes, evangelical faith, and miracles. They are designed to capture the imaginations of readers and transport them into the world that is soon, fatefully, to unfold. The original novel depicts passengers flying on a Boeing 747 who suddenly and without warning disappear from their seats. But this is only one isolated scene. Simultaneously, confusion, terror, and chaos spread throughout the world as born-again Christians are "raptured" into heaven and the rest of humanity is left behind to face waves of tribulation and unimaginable suffering.

AN ESCAPIST THEOLOGY

As worldwide sales indicate, this story line makes for gripping drama. But it is more than just a "good read"; it is shaping minds and creating assumptions about faith and the future. This end-of-the-world approach is having a profound emotional, spiritual, *and* political impact on Christians and other religious seekers throughout the world. In recent surveys, more than 50 percent of people in the United States believe that the world will soon come to a catastrophic end. The more compelling question, however, is whether this is a healthy indicator or simply a numbing, escapist state of mind. It is one thing to have this end-time scenario offered as creative fiction or as a form of religious entertainment. But these novels are presented as much more than that. They reinforce a belief system that distorts the message of Scripture and, in addition, creates a way of approaching contemporary human history that is dangerous and ultimately irresponsible. The following points reflect some basic arguments against these theologies of "rapture."

First, they are based on an uncritical, partial reading of Scripture, in particular, selected passages from Ezekiel, Daniel, Mark, and the Book of Revelation. Most mainstream Christians, including Protestant, Catholic, and Orthodox, are committed to reading the Bible not only in its text, but also in its *con*-text—in other words, taking into account the form of literature, the historical situation, and the theological purpose of the author or authors. Lindsey, LaHaye, Jenkins, and fundamentalist evangelicals like Jerry Falwell, John Hagee, and Pat Robertson, take the sacred writings and force them into a mold designed to justify their theological assumptions and their cultural, political ideologies.

Second, they foster a fear-based faith that views God's justice as retributive and vengeful. For those who claim to have the certainty of being "born again" and thereby assured of salvation, there is likely some consolation in such an approach. Perhaps it would be more correct to describe it as a form of religious complacency, since it represents spiritual assurance at the expense of the rest of humanity, especially the poor; the starving children; the victims of AIDS, earthquakes, and tsunamis; and the growing numbers of refugees of wars. "Rapture and Armageddon scenarios," writes New Testament scholar Barbara Rossing, "tap into Americans' love for disaster films and survivalist plots. Readers of end-time novels readily envision themselves among the few who will escape planetary disaster."[2]

Third, this is a religion of escapism, not of Christian responsibility. It calls us not to authentic conversion or communal commitment but to a narrow, self-centered pursuit of individual salvation. In the language of American consumerism, we might describe it as taking out an "eternal life insurance policy." The late-nineteenth-century evangelist Dwight L. Moody, speaking of the end-times, once asked his congregation, "Why polish the brass on a sinking ship?"[3] His question is noteworthy on several levels. It presupposes an otherworldly view of faith. It also presumes that the primary role of Christianity, even in good times, is to perform regular maintenance for the dominant culture, to keep the normalcy of structural injustice "shipshape" while the "righteous" sail toward heaven. But if the end is near, then even this politically passive role becomes superfluous. If this world is soon to end in a fiery catastrophe, why bother to work for justice? Why put effort into working to overcome poverty or war? Why develop responsible programs of research and societal restructuring to reverse global warming and improve the environment? If this world is to be destroyed by God's wrath, what else is there to do except read our Bibles and stay away from nonbelievers?

Finally, it is not just that biblical fundamentalism is escapist. What makes this perspective—even as entertaining fiction—truly dangerous is that it invites believers to support systems of violence. The glorious return of the "warrior Christ" relies on creating the historical conditions for Armageddon, namely, supporting the buildup of nuclear weapons, opposing a long-range peace between Israel and Palestine, and fostering an atmosphere of suspicion, even disdain for nonbelievers. Instead of heeding the call to confront injustice and work for peace, this ideology, in effect, maintains that the task of Christians is to fuel the forces of division and hostility. True believers are encouraged to pray for the end of the world. Worse still, they are expected to pay for the coming apocalypse with their (our) tax dollars, at the expense of the poor and the starving. From my perspective, this is the opposite of the preaching and practice of Jesus. It is an assault on the vision of the Beatitudes and a contradiction to the gospel.

CHRISTIAN REALISM AND THE REALITY OF WAR

Mainline Christians, including Protestant, Orthodox, and Roman Catholic, believe in a second coming of Christ. In the Gospel of Mark, Jesus gives us this simple advice: "But about that day or hour no one knows, neither the angels in heaven, nor the Son, but only the Father" (13:32). When the risen Christ did not come as anticipated, believers began developing interpretations of history and the role of the church in the world. For example, theologians have continued to make a distinction between individual and universal eschatology. The former refers to the inevitable day that each of us will die. On a personal level this is our "end-time"—our experience of mortality and our encounter with God in the mystery of transcendence. Universal eschatology, on the other hand, explores the destiny toward which all of created time and space is moving. It is concerned with the goal of creation as a whole, including our call to "till and to keep" our planet, to work toward human community by confronting injustice, and to create the "things that make for peace."

The earliest communities of Christians believed that the second coming of Christ was going to occur soon. They were mistaken in their timing but not in their ultimate vision of hope. It is almost two thousand years since the dying and rising of Jesus, so Christian theologians have long since explored the open-ended nature of time. While there have always been those who predicted the imminent end of the world, most believers live with the conviction that we are called to embrace history as a gift and a responsibility. We focus on the inherent goodness of time and the prophetic task of creating a more just human community.

If time is open-ended, what does it mean to work for "the things that make for peace"? For the church this has a varied and mixed history. The emergence of the monastic movement in the early Middle Ages, and the religious communities of evangelical poverty have been a strong witness of charity and solidarity with the poor. The Catholic Church has a long and credible history of teaching and practicing commutative justice and service to the poor. On the other hand, it has only been in the last century that the institutional church has begun to confront the forms of systemic injustice that are often a function of governments and their leaders. When we look more specifically at the role of the church in creating the structures of justice and working for peace, the picture is, at best, ambivalent. In this area, the church's participation has sometimes involved as much compromise as prophetic action.

There are many contemporary church leaders who claim—along the lines of Reinhold Niebuhr—that this is simply Christian realism. Even though we are committed to the gospel of peace, we recognize the need, in certain circumstances, for a "just war." As far back as St. Augustine, Christianity has struggled to describe the conditions that make war in the pursuit of peace justified. It is not my intention here to engage in the complex debate surrounding this issue, except to recognize that there are legitimate arguments on both sides.

What is clear, however, is that there are profound difficulties in applying the just war principles to actual historical circumstances. Just war theories were developed before the Crusades and the feudal societies of the Middle Ages. With the advent of modern warfare, such theories have become even more difficult to utilize or enforce. The presumption of Christianity, most theologians continue to maintain, is against war. War is only a last resort and then it must be for a just cause and carried out in a way that respects the safety of noncombatants.

Like so many human realities, the theory is clearer than its application. For one thing, governments can use propaganda, even outright lies, to rationalize the need to go to war. Church leaders often fail to question the motives and information given by those who have political power. And once combat has begun, all those involved are immersed in "the fog of war"[4]—the chaos and the ambiguity that surround every military conflict. Simply stated, it is increasingly difficult, if not impossible, to separate combatants and noncombatants. Once military action has begun, there are few ways in which the principle of proportionality can be enforced. Given modern weapons, how is it possible to make the human and other costs of war commensurate with the values at stake and the evil that one is trying to overcome?

THE DEMANDS OF THE GOSPEL

Over the last decades, in settings ranging from supermarkets to airport terminals, well-meaning people have asked me if I am a Christian. I have become increasingly uncomfortable with this question. What I understand as the call to faith and service is often not what most of these well-intentioned people are assuming. Who *is* a Christian? And what does it mean to believe in and live the gospel in our polarized culture? The answers to these questions are often varied and contradictory.

We live in a time of unparalleled upheaval and historical transformation. At times of radical change, people tend to seek simple solutions and unambiguous answers. Thus, many believing Christians appear to want Jesus to be the answer, not the question. They prefer their religion to arrive in gift wrapping. They expect it to give them security and comfort, to reinforce their assumptions and confirm their political outlook. They want clarity, not confusion; commandments, not suggestions; biblical certainties, not challenging parables.

A number of recent polls indicate that fundamentalist Christianity (and other forms of religious fundamentalism) is growing, while mainstream Christian traditions are in decline. Sociologically, this is understandable in that traditional forms of Christian practice tend to become more stable and fixed in their practice and less open to change. What many people do not realize, however, is that fundamentalist Christian movements are really not that traditional or, for that matter, not that fundamental. They combine the best of contemporary marketing strategies with a reactionary political version of the gospel. In an individualistic, consumerist culture this message sells. It is remarkably—and not surprisingly—successful.

The disturbing part is that many Catholic and Protestant leaders are looking at what is happening in the fundamentalist churches and are advocating that mainline traditions ought to learn from them. They are suggesting that mainstream Christian churches should return to a more literalist understanding of Scripture, clear dogmatic statements, and the exclusion of those who are "other." In a time of fear, this may appear to be an effective "business model" for marketing and increasing membership, but it isn't necessarily the prophetic summons of the gospel. Christianity is intended to be good news, but it has never been "easy news." It cannot be reshaped to fit the self-help programs that flood our bookstores or the religious "success models" that proclaim the good life of capitalism as our religious privilege or our graced inheritance.

What are the things that make for peace? Jesus did not give us a political manifesto to answer this question. Nor did he leave us with a short list of practical suggestions. He simply confronted the structures of systemic violence and bore the consequences of his choices. Perhaps the things that make for peace are the same for us—in the unique, complex circumstances in which we live and seek community. Clearly, it has something to do with confronting our inner attitudes of violence, as well as challenging the systemic injustice that surrounds us. This is simply another way of saying that we are called to follow the crucified and risen Christ. His words continue to haunt us and to invite us: "If any want to become my followers, let them deny themselves and take up their cross daily and follow me" (Luke 9:23).

14

Pursuing Peace

Justice as the Nonviolent Coming of God

Nonviolence is the greatest force at the disposal of humankind. It is mightier than the mightiest weapon of destruction.
> —Mahatma Gandhi

The Peace Corps left today and my heart sank low. The danger is extreme and they were right to leave. . . . Now I must assess my own position, because I am not up for suicide. Several times I have decided to leave El Salvador. I almost could, except for the children, the poor, bruised victims of this insanity. Who would care for them? Whose heart could be so staunch as to favor the reasonable thing in a sea of their tears and loneliness? Not mine, dear friend, not mine.
> —Jean Donovan

On December 2, 1980, three Maryknoll Sisters, Dorothy Kazel, Maura Clarke, Ita Ford, and lay missioner Jean Donovan were followed and then attacked on a desolate road in El Salvador by five Salvadoran National Guardsmen in plainclothes. The four women were tortured, raped, murdered, and buried in a shallow grave. *Roses in December*, a film documentary completed in 1982, begins with footage of the brutalized bodies of these women being exhumed from that desolate grave. These courageous women, working for justice among the poor, were noncombatants killed in the early phase of what would become a brutal war between an American-backed junta and leftist rebels, a war that would leave tens of thousands dead.

What are the things that make for peace? I return again to this compelling question, haunted by the scene of Jesus' weeping over Jerusalem in Luke's Gospel, and aware of the mysterious way it converges with the scene in El Salvador in 1980. When the news of that brutal violence reached the rest of the world, I believe that the body of Christ wept again—this time over the city of humankind. What are the things that make for peace? Should we be seeking the consummation of history as it is described in the end-time scenarios of *The Late Great Planet Earth* or the novels of the Left Behind series? There is a great deal of ambiguity in our human journey, but for me the answer to this question is as clear as the sunrise on a bright morning. No, the fundamentalist end-time explanation is not what will make for peace. If anything, it constitutes a betrayal of the gospel and of our commitment to follow Christ.

Are the tasks of peace to be found in the further development of sophisticated instruments of war, including more nuclear weapons, as a deterrent to evil? Is our primary ethical commitment related to discerning when and under what conditions military conflict in the pursuit of peace is justified? Answering these questions is more difficult, but, on a personal level, it is no less clear. In response to the first question, there is growing consensus, even among those who adhere to theories of a just war, that the further buildup of weapons of mass destruction will not deter, but may even precipitate the very catastrophe that we are seeking to avoid. In regard to the second question, my reflections lead me to think as a realist but to choose as a disciple of the nonviolent Christ. While I respect that there are situations in which military intervention (with the support and authority of the United Nations) may at times be necessary to protect innocent lives, I do not believe that these concerns should be the central focus of our political endeavors.

What, then, should lay claim to our ethical commitment? What *are* the things that make for peace? Our first priority, I believe, is the task of confronting the systems of injustice and helping to create practical pathways toward solidarity and equality in the human community. It is related to the kind of service in which the four courageous women were engaged when the death squads tracked them down and brutally ended their lives. The call of the gospel is as practical and concrete today as it was in the hills and villages of Galilee at the time of Jesus. These women were following that same call in the back roads and towns of El Salvador.

Does this imply that we should leave our jobs, our families, and our homes and sign up to serve in developing countries as justice workers? I don't think so. As I stated earlier, the first thing that the people of those nations would likely tell us is: Don't come here until or unless you are willing to confront the structures of injustice in your own society. "Choose to live simply," Elizabeth Ann Seton writes, "in order that others may simply live." They probably would also remind us that we don't have to go to El Salvador, to Darfur, or even to the south side of Chicago to struggle against violence and injustice. We need to face the viper's tangle of oppression that already envelops us, and to think and act in ways that confront these systems.

We don't have to become missioners to live the gospel. Over the years, this is a lesson I have learned—and am still learning—more out of experience and humility than out of courage. The story of the four women in El Salvador is a flashpoint in my memory. It shapes and challenges my life, perhaps because I journeyed in their world briefly—and it changed my life. In June of 1976, I had the privilege of spending almost a month in El Salvador. Ostensibly, I was there to lead a retreat with Franciscan sisters who were living and working among the poor and by their presence confronting the oppressive structures of that society's wealth and power. In reality I was there to listen and to learn; to listen to the people in whatever ways I was able, given my limited language skills; and to learn from both the people and the missioners who were in solidarity with them.

After I returned home, I became aware of three important realities. First, their ministry is beyond my stamina, and certainly beyond my courage. Whatever my convictions and ideals, I cannot do what they are doing. In Jean Donovan's apt phrase in the above epigraph, I have chosen "the reasonable thing." I returned to my life and my work in a relatively safe part of this precarious world. Second, what they are doing is close to the heart of the gospel. It is a front-line form of discipleship, the most authentic witness to the things that make for peace. Finally, I am convinced that I must continue to find ways to support them and to walk my own path of discipleship by committing myself to parallel forms of justice making in my daily life.

JUSTICE AS THE PATHWAY TO PEACE

The four women in El Salvador are a metaphor for a movement. In the last sixty years, a quiet, resilient energy has emerged among Christian believers and other advocates for justice. This movement is ecumenical and interreligious. It is made up of women and men, young and old. It comprises diverse races and ethnic groups from all socioeconomic backgrounds, including grassroots small communities among the poor. It is reflected in the *comunidades eclesiales de base* in Central and South America; it is embodied in the worker cooperatives and justice communities in Africa and Asia; and it is stirring in small faith and action groups in the United States and Europe. Over the decades these intentional communities have been joined by an emerging cadre of theologians (a growing number of whom are women) who give voice to these grassroots stirrings and help shape the emerging vision of justice and peacemaking. This movement does not have a centralized authority or a single designation. It does not have an international organization, because it is made up of many movements and organizations with similar goals and commitments.

What do these justice movements have in common? They reject the escapist, fear-based, end-time scenarios of fundamentalist Christians. They are equally dissatisfied with the focus of some church leaders and their followers who are preoccupied with studying how, when, and under what conditions we are justified in going to war. Instead, they are concentrating on the challenges of restorative justice that will make for genuine peace. I am speaking here of the thousands of dedicated people who have given their lives—in martyrdom or in the quiet self-gift of daily service—to live in solidarity with the poor, to empower the oppressed, to educate the illiterate, to confront political systems of structural violence, to heal the sick, to journey with the dying, and to stand in prophetic challenge against those who would destroy the rain forests or deepen the already widening gap between the rich and the poor on our beleaguered planet.

Many of us recognize the familiar leaders in these movements: Mohandas Gandhi, Maria Corazón Aquino, Desmond Tutu, Nelson Mandela, the Dalai Lama, Aung San Suu Kyi, Martin Luther King, Rosa Parks, Oscar Romero, Teresa of Calcutta, to name only a few. Some of us may recognize others who are also models in their commitment to justice: Helen Prejean, James Baldwin, Dorothy Stang, Franz Jägerstätter, Helen Caldicott, Lech Wałęsa, Mary Robinson, Dietrich Bonhoeffer, Indira Gandhi, Daniel and Philip Berrigan, Greg Mortenson, Dianna Ortiz, the four women martyrs of El Salvador, César Chávez, Kofi Annan, the eight Jesuit martyrs of El Salvador and their housekeeper and her young daughter. These are only a few of those who are part of a wide, surging river of justice makers.

There are also outstanding justice communities and organizations, including thousands who are members of missionary communities and other ecumenical or interreligious groups who are laying down their lives to empower the poor at home or in developing nations. We can find a similar spirit of commitment in Maryknoll, Catholic Worker houses, Sojourners, national and international Commissions on Truth and Reconciliation, Pax Christi, the Community of Sant'Egidio, Network, the Ground Zero Center for Nonviolent Action, the Jesuit Volunteer Corps, the Fellowship of Reconciliation, the Southern Poverty Law Center, Médecins Sans Frontières, the American Friends Service Committee, the Center of Concern, Catholic Relief Services, Caritas Internationalis, and many others.

THE NONVIOLENT COMING OF GOD

In 1997, at the 23rd Eucharistic Congress in Bologna, Italy, Bob Dylan was invited to sing his popular folk song "Blowin' in the Wind." After Dylan had finished performing, Pope John Paul II—who was presiding at the gathering—told the crowd of three hundred thousand young Catholics that the answer to life's questions is indeed blowing in the wind. He reminded them, however, that it is not a wind that destroys things or blows them away, but rather "the wind that is the breath and voice of the Spirit." In these final reflections, I reflect on this "wind of the Spirit," this resilient presence, the creative inner force that is urging us to work for justice in the long road toward peace.

Consider this intriguing question. *What if the second coming of Christ is neither an imminent global catastrophe nor a distant apocalyptic event, but rather an unfolding process within human history?* What if Jesus' return is not so much something that we are to wait for, as it is a creative endeavor in which we are already involved through our commitment to create a human community marked by justice? The community of believers—and humanity as a whole—is the expansion of the body of Christ in time and space. We usually think of the church—the people of God—as having a mission. On one level this may indeed be the case. But perhaps it is more correct to say that Jesus *is* the mission of God, and that the crucified and risen Christ has a community to carry out his mission, his work of transforming our broken world into a healed planet, a restored abode of understanding and peace.

Contemporary church teaching invites us to understand the future of humanity in this light:

> Far from diminishing our concern to develop this earth, the expectancy of a new earth should spur us on, for it is here that the body of a new human family grows, foreshadowing in some way the age which is still to come. That is why, although we must be careful to distinguish earthly progress clearly from the increase of the kingdom of Christ, such progress is of vital concern to the kingdom of God, insofar as it can contribute to the better ordering of human society.[1]

There are also an increasing number of theologians who are describing our present crisis and our future task in terms of our responsibility to embody the justice of God and make visible the peace of the Spirit. The heading for these final reflections is taken from the visionary book by James W. Douglass, *The Nonviolent Coming of God*.[2] There are several themes in contemporary theology that ground this vision and make it credible and compelling.

Creation as the Sacrament of God

The first premise is that creation is an unfinished symphony. Our vast, unfolding universe is God's work in progress; it is our creator's ongoing sacrament of self-expression, gratuity, and freedom. Consider the following possibility for a creative "night out." Instead of going to see a film or to listen to a concert, take in the cosmos. Some evening after sunset, go somewhere beyond the city lights so that you can see the Milky Way as it stretches across our sky against the background of deeper space. You don't need a telescope or a star map, just the willingness to stand in wonder and to contemplate the mystery that envelops us. Our cosmos is immense and expansive beyond our ability to comprehend. And, since we human beings have become what Teilhard de Chardin describes as "the arrow of evolution," we share in the task of reaching toward deeper liberation, toward more conscious, generative life.

This 13.7-billion-year journey has found privileged expression on our tiny, luminous planet. Holy communion is already realized in creation, even as it is more deeply expressed in the breaking of the bread and the sharing of the eucharistic cup. There are likely other centers of life and self-consciousness in the universe, but we have yet to discover them. What we do know is that God found this creation to be inherently good. So good that—in our limited way of expressing it—our creator embraced our universe in the mystery of the incarnation. The eternal, creative Word continues to become one with us in the unfolding of awareness and freedom. This truth stands in contradiction to any theology that envisions this planet as ending in a convulsion of violence—whether this is by divine vengeance or human irresponsibility.

Jesus and the New Humanity

The second theme is related to the way in which we view Jesus. For many Christians, over the centuries, the emphasis has been on Jesus as the Son of God—precisely in his power as *divine*—coming to save humanity from its sins. But Jesus is also human, and he liberates us by embracing and transforming our humanity. He became our savior, by becoming, in the first place, our brother. In the Gospel accounts Jesus avoids the terms "messiah" or "son of God" as self-designations. When Jesus refers to himself he almost invariably uses the expression "the son of man." In Aramaic this expression, *bar enasha*, is usually translated as "a human being." According to Walter Wink, "the implication seems to be that Jesus intentionally avoided honorific titles, and preferred to be known simply as 'the man' or the 'human being.' Apparently he saw his task as helping people become more truly human."[3]

In his solidarity with the blind, the lame, the imprisoned, the paralyzed, the leprous, the mentally ill, and the social outcasts, Jesus is already signaling the pathway toward becoming the "new humanity." Any community that reaches out to its most vulnerable members with inclusive love and liberating justice is embodying this same vision. Just as Jesus was transformed through his nonviolent, suffering service, so too will the emerging new humanity be transformed through its solidarity and self-emptying on behalf of those who are oppressed. "The Human Being that Jesus shows us by the example of his life," writes James Douglass, "must suffer and die so that a new humanity will rise."[4]

The Power of Nonviolent Love

As difficult as it is for most of us to believe, it is becoming clear that the liberating presence of God can come more alive in our world only if we intentionally choose to live nonviolent lives in the service of the gospel. This involves a daily choice—in our personal, interpersonal, and communal lives—to embody what Gandhi calls *satyagraha*, or the nonviolent power of love and service. For centuries the nonviolence that Jesus preached and practiced in the Gospel accounts has been ignored or explained away, either as an ideal beyond our reach or as a personal way of life separate from the larger social and political systems that rule the world. Several leading theologians of the twentieth and twenty-first centuries, including John Howard Yoder, Dorothee Soelle, Stanley Hauerwas, María Pilar Aquino, Jon Sobrino, Pheme Perkins, Walter Wink, James Douglass, and others, have made it clear that Jesus' teaching and practice of nonviolence were not a private choice, but a gospel mandate. It is urgent that our Christian communities reclaim this vision. It is, at the very least, an ideal to be seriously pursued, even in the face of discussions surrounding the justified use of military interventions to protect the rights of the oppressed.

Not of This World?

In the Gospel of John (18:28-40), Jesus is brought before Pilate and asked whether or not he is a king. His response is forthright. It is also widely misunderstood. "My kingdom is not from this world. If my kingdom were from this world, my followers would be fighting to keep me from being handed over to the Jews. But as it is, my kingdom is not from here" (18:36). This encounter between Pilate and Jesus is a confrontation between empire and gospel, between the normalcy of systemic violence and the "dangerous and subversive memory" of Jesus of Nazareth. This confrontation also raises haunting questions. Why, for instance, did Jesus not declare a just war and command his followers to fight against the Roman legions? Why did he not lead a righteous revolution?

To respond to these questions, we need to make an important clarification regarding Jesus' use of the terms "this world" and "here." Over the centuries Christians have interpreted Jesus' words to mean that his kingdom is in heaven or, in other words, not here on earth. It is in the world to come, not in this one. So the "here," according to this interpretation, is not the creation that God has given us—not this holy ground and rolling seas, not this teeming community, not this time and space in the unfolding cosmos.

It is clear, however, from the rest of the Gospel accounts, especially in Jesus' teaching regarding the kingdom, that this is not the case. The kingdom of God is already breaking into history. It is as near as our breathing, as close as our heartbeat, as present as our family or the stranger we meet on the street. The kingdom that Jesus proclaims encompasses our lives. What Jesus is telling the procurator—and each of us—is that his kingdom is not of *Pilate*'s world— not of the world of empire and political control. Jesus' kingdom has no part in governing by expedient brutality, no part in the world of systemic oppression, no place in the structures that create poverty and hopelessness. But let us not be mistaken. This alternate kingdom is nevertheless *here*—already unfolding in the scourged body and crowned head of the man of sorrows. Here, in the diverse, global reach of humanity.

In John's Gospel there are two meanings for "this world." One refers to creation, as in, "God so loved the world . . ." (3:12); the second describes the world of human culture and contrivance. The latter is the world of systemic violence and oppression created by the powerful and sometimes blessed by the religious institutions that have been co-opted from their call to solidarity with the poor. When Jesus says his kingdom is not of this world, he is referring to the world of empire, the system of violence that goes under the name of civilization, but whose normal expression includes the exploitation of the poor by the rich, and the abuse of the vulnerable by the powerful. Jesus' kingdom is certainly not of this system. Jesus refused to become part of these structures of oppressive power. He invites us to stand against the same darkness. And, at the same time, he calls us to commit ourselves to the healing of the human community.

The End of the World

Most biblical scholars have concluded that Jesus believed in and preached the coming end of the world. The lingering question is,

Which world? To what sphere of existence was he referring? In what many commentators refer to as Mark's "little apocalypse"(Mark 13), the author is writing in the aftermath of the Jewish revolt of 66-74 CE that destroyed the temple and brought the full, savage retaliation of the Roman legions down upon the Jewish people. In these verses Jesus voices his premonition that Jerusalem and the people, given their refusal to walk the road of nonviolent resistance, would face inevitable devastation.

Those who survived the massacres and widespread destruction were shaken to the core. Their faith was flooded with doubt. The cry of their hearts and the question in their minds was: Where is Jesus? Why did he not return in glory and power? Where was he during the agony of his people? Perhaps that is why Mark describes the betrayal, the denial, the mockery, the agony, and the abandonment that Jesus experienced in such stark detail. This is precisely the form of suffering and death that thousands of Jewish believers experienced at the hands of the Roman soldiers.[5] The temple had been destroyed. Its role as the central symbol of Judaism was finished. For many Jews the world had indeed come to an end, not as they had hoped or anticipated but as Jesus had dreaded and painfully foretold.

Did Jesus also have a wider, more inclusive vision of the end of time and the consummation of history? The scholarly debate around this issue will likely continue, but the vision we are addressing here is beyond that discussion. Jesus was speaking of an entirely different "end of the world," namely, the end of the systems of evil and injustice. He is referring to what Walter Wink aptly describes as "the dismantling of the Powers"—the normalcy of violence in civilization, the structures of oppression that grind the poor into the ground and take advantage of the vulnerable, the innocent, and the meek. Jesus is saying, in effect, that his second coming is already under way. It is taking place each time someone stands up against violence. It is present each time someone who has been abused responds by choosing the long road toward healing. It is unfolding in the martyrs of justice and the courage of peacemakers. It is stirring in the individuals and communities that choose to love their enemies and pray for their persecutors. The world of injustice is coming to an end wherever the force of love is greater than the raging chaos of vengeance. Violence ends when courage stands quietly and calmly with the eyes of truth.

Hope: Gift and Choice

For those of us who believe in the crucified and risen One—the cosmic Christ—this is a hopeful *and* a demanding vision. It does not appear that injustice will be defeated anytime soon, or that the world of violence is about to end. Perhaps this is precisely the challenge of discipleship in our time—to trust that our prayer and action on behalf of justice will make a difference despite all indications to the contrary. It is possible that, in the first decades of the twenty-first century, believing has less to do with doctrinal details and more to do with embodying the gospel vision, even when it is not politically correct or religiously approved. Perhaps, like the carpenter from Nazareth, we must choose to live and act without the assurance of significant outcomes or measurable results.

Like most of my sisters and brothers in the human community, I do not have a clear view of the future—no magic lantern, no crystal ball, no personal revelation, no apocalyptic secret. But, whatever the future will be, this is what I trust. The nonviolent coming of God is unfolding as surely as scattered seeds will find good soil, as certainly as there is hidden treasure in the field of human history, and as confidently as grains of wheat fall into the ground in search of a harvest that is still to come.

Hope has feet. And we are still walking.

Acknowledgments

The reflections in this book have been maturing for many years. They are the outcome of circles of relationships, ministry, dialogue, and community reaching as far back as the 1960s. They emerge from the ministry that I was privileged to share with friends and colleagues as a college teacher, campus minister, social justice advocate, pastor, and—during the last twenty-five years—as an adjunct university instructor and a psychotherapist working with survivors of sexual abuse, domestic violence, and other forms of healing from injustice.

There are far more people who have shaped my life with their courage and resilience than I can begin to acknowledge. I can only offer them my gratitude as sisters and brothers on the same journey.

In addition to my family and closest friends, I am grateful to Eugene C. Kennedy for his mentoring and ongoing friendship since he taught me psychology as an undergraduate. I recall with gratitude the impact of Roland Murphy, O. Carm., who made the Hebrew Scriptures come alive, and John Tracy Ellis, who gave church history a scholarly grounding and a pastoral perspective.

It has been a privilege to share ministry with the Franciscan Sisters of Perpetual Adoration at Viterbo College (now Viterbo University) in La Crosse, Wisconsin. They supported my commitment to teach a course on justice and peace in the early 1970s. I am likewise indebted to Bishop Frederick W. Freking, who appointed me as the first director of the Office of Justice and Peace for the Diocese of La Crosse in 1976. I especially want to thank Bishop John J. Paul for his support and trust over the years. During this same period, the Justice and Peace Commission brought together a community of prophetic people, including Jeanne Conzemius, SSJ-TOSF, Audrey Olson, CSJ, Judy Kramer, OSB, and Mike Brown, all of whom were gifted directors. These efforts also included the vital leadership of Ray Stroik, Kathy Smith, Leo and Janet Jacoby, Jim Birnbaum, Greg Speltz, and many others from whom I have learned so much about the gospel vision of justice.

During the last twenty-five years of ministry in the Pacific Northwest, I am especially grateful to Archbishop Raymond Hunthausen for his vision, his courage, and his support. This book is gratefully dedicated to him. I am also indebted to my colleagues and students in the School of Theology and Ministry at Seattle University, the former staff members of Therapy and Renewal Associates, Phil Wallace, and my other friends in Seattle. I also want to thank several communities of religious women and men for their support and encouragement: the Sisters of Providence in the Pacific Northwest, the Franciscan Friars of California, the Holy Cross Sisters and their community in Bangladesh, the Benedictine Sisters of St Bede, the Maryknoll Sisters, Brothers, priests, and lay associates, and many others.

I am grateful to my editor/publisher, Michael Leach, for his encouragement, advice, support—and patience.

Finally, I want to thank my dear friend and longtime colleague, Fran Ferder, FSPA, for the gift of shared ministry and our mutual commitment to justice.

Notes

INTRODUCTION

1. Unless otherwise noted, biblical quotations are from the NRSV. Quotations from the Jerusalem Bible (JB) are from *The Jerusalem Bible* (London: Darton, Longman & Todd, 1966). Quotations from the J. B. Phillips translation are from J. B. Phillips, *The New Testament in Modern English* (New York: Macmillan, 1962).

2. For a more extended study of this issue, see, for example, Bruce B. Lawrence, *Shattering the Myth: Islam beyond Violence* (1998; repr., Princeton, N.J.: Princeton University Press, 2006); or Karen Armstrong, *Islam: A Short History* (New York: Alfred A. Knopf, 1993).

3. Synod of Bishops, 1971, *Justice in the World* (Washington, D.C.: United States Conference of Catholic Bishops, 1972), #6 (emphasis added).

1. ENCOUNTERING A GOD OF LIBERATION

1. Pierre Teilhard de Chardin, *The Future of Man,* trans. Norman Denny (New York: Harper & Row, 1964), 11-13. In a different context, I referenced this same image in a previous book, *Our Journey toward God* (Chicago: Thomas More, 1977), 71-73.

2. Loren C. Eiseley, *The Immense Journey: An Imaginative Naturalist Explores the Mysteries of Man and Nature* (New York: Random House, 1956).

3. See especially John F. Haught, *Deeper than Darwin: The Prospect for Religion in the Age of Evolution* (Boulder, Colo.: Westview, 2003); idem, *God after Darwin: A Theology of Evolution,* 2nd ed. (Boulder, Colo.: Westview, 2008).

4. In Carter Phipps, "A Theologian of Renewal: The Evolutionary Spirituality of John F. Haught," *EnlightenNext* Issue 42 (December 2008-February 2009): 66.

5. See, for example, Diarmuid Ó'Murchú, *Ancestral Grace: Meeting God in Our Human Story* (Maryknoll, N.Y.: Orbis Books, 2008).

6. Brian Swimme and Thomas Berry, *The Universe Story: From the Primordial Flaring Forth to the Ecozoic Era—A Celebration of the Unfolding of the Cosmos* (San Francisco: HarperSanFrancisco, 1992), 5.

7. Joseph Campbell, as quoted in an interview with Eugene C. Kennedy, in *The Now and Future Church: The Psychology of Being an American Catholic* (Garden City, N.Y.: Doubleday, 1984), 87.

8. Ibid., 85 (emphasis added).

2. TURNING DREAMS TO ASHES

1. Elie Wiesel, *Night,* trans. Stella Rodway (New York: Hill & Wang, 1960; repr., New York: Bantam Books, 1982).

2. Eckhart Tolle, *A New Earth: Awakening to Your Life's Purpose* (New York: Dutton/Penguin, 2006), 11-12.

3. United States Holocaust Memorial Museum, «The Holocaust,» *Holocaust Encyclopedia,* http://www.ushmm.org/wlc/en/index.php?ModuleId=10005143 (accessed June 9, 2009).

4. An example of this approach is Guenter Lewy, "Were American Indians the Victims of Genocide?" *Commentary* (September 2004), 55-63.

5. United States Holocaust Memorial Museum, "The Holocaust," *Holocaust Encyclopedia* (see reference in n. 3 above).

6. For a more detailed description of genocide in Rwanda, see Gérard Prunier, *The Rwanda Crisis: History of Genocide* (New York: Columbia University Press, 1995).

7. *Fourth Annual Report of the International Criminal Tribunal for Rwanda to the UN General Assembly,* September 1999, http://www.ictrcaselaw.org/docs/N9925571.pdf, 6, #16.

8. See Nicholas D. Kristof, "The World Capital of Killing," *New York Times,* February 7, 2010.

9. See, for example, Jack Miles, *God: A Biography* (New York: Alfred A. Knopf, 1995); Karen Armstrong, *A History of God: The 4,000-Year Quest of Judaism, Christianity, and Islam* (New York: Alfred A. Knopf, 1993); Robert Wright, *The Evolution of God* (New York: Little, Brown, 2009).

10. Armstrong, *History of God*, xx.

11. Miles, *God: A Biography;* see, for example, 154-59.

12. Armstrong, *History of God*, 18-19.

13. W. H. Auden, "The Age of Anxiety," *Collected Poems*, ed. Edward Mendelson (New York: Random House, 1976), 407.

14. John G. Neihardt, *Black Elk Speaks: Being the Life Story of a Holy Man of the Oglala Sioux as Told through John G. Neihardt* (1932; repr., Lincoln: University of Nebraska Press, 1968), 20-47, here 43.

15. Ibid., 43 n. 8.

16. This saying was first found in a pseudo-Hermetic treatise of the twelfth century and later attributed variously to Alain de Lille, Giordano Bruno, and Blaise Pascal. See Frances A. Yates, *Giordano Bruno and the Hermetic Tradition* (Chicago: University of Chicago Press, 1964), 247.

17. Martin Buber, *I and Thou*, trans. Walter Kaufmann (1970; repr., New York: Scribner, 1996).

3. Confronting Violence

1. Walter Brueggemann, *The Prophetic Imagination* (Philadelphia: Fortress, 1978), 13 (emphasis in original).

2. Ibid., 13-15.

3. Karen Armstrong, *The Great Transformation: The Beginning of Our Religious Traditions* (New York: Alfred A. Knopf, 2006); see especially xi-xviii, and 367-99.

4. John Dominic Crossan, *God and Empire: Jesus against Rome, Then and Now* (San Francisco: HarperSanFrancisco, 2007), 57.

5. Ibid.

6. Willigis Jäger, *Search for the Meaning of Life: Essays and Reflections on the Mystical Experience* (Liguori, Mo.: Triumph Books, 1995), 44-45. See also Ken Wilbur, *Up from Eden: A Transpersonal View of Human Evolution* (Garden City, N.Y.: Doubleday, 1981), 297.

7. In this section I am indebted to "A New Axial Age," an interview with Karen Armstrong conducted by Jessica Roemischer, in *EnlightenNext* Issue 31 (December 2005-February 2006).

8. Armstrong, *Great Transformation*, xiii-xiv.

9. *Gaudium et Spes* (The Pastoral Constitution on the Church in the Modern World), in *Vatican Council II: Constitutions, Decrees, and Declarations*, ed. Austin Flannery, O.P. (Northport, N.Y.: Costello, 1996).

4. Challenging Systems of Injustice

1. Dom Helder Camara, *The Spiral of Violence*, trans. Della Couling (Denville, N.J.: Dimension Books, 1971).

2. John Dominic Crossan, *God and Empire: Jesus against Rome, Then and Now* (San Francisco: HarperSanFrancisco, 2007), 29.

3. Ibid., 30.

4. One of the early, controversial books in this genre is Howard Zinn, *A People's History of the United States: 1492–Present* (20th Anniversary Edition; New York: HarperCollins, 1999).

5. Crossan, *God and Empire*, 30.

6. Michael Hardt and Antonio Negri, *Empire* (Cambridge, Mass.: Harvard University Press, 2000).

7. Walter Wink, *Naming the Powers: The Language of Power in the New Testament* (Philadelphia: Fortress, 1984); *Unmasking the Powers: The Invisible Forces That Determine Human Existence* (Philadelphia: Fortress, 1986); *Engaging the Powers: Discernment and Resistance in a World of Domination* (Minneapolis: Fortress, 1992).

8. Walter Wink, *The Powers That Be: Theology for a New Millennium* (New York: Doubleday, 1998), 27.

9. Ibid., 28.

10. Ibid., 39.

11. Ibid., 31.

12. Nicholas D. Kristof and Sheryl WuDunn, *Half the Sky: Turning Oppression into Opportunity for Women Worldwide* (New York: Alfred A. Knopf, 2009).

13. Ibid., xvii.

14. Greg Mortenson, with David Oliver Relin, *Three Cups of Tea: One Man's Mission to Promote Peace—One School at a Time* (New York: Penguin Books, 2007); *Stones into Schools: Promoting Peace with Books, Not Bombs, in Afghanistan and Pakistan* (New York: Viking, 2009).

5. SEEKING JUSTICE

1. The transliteration of these words from the Hebrew varies. Some scholars use *mišpaṭ* and *ṣedeq/ṣedaqa* in their transliterations.

2. Other biblical examples might include Gen 18:19; 1 Kgs 10:9; Pss 89:14; 119:121; Isa 9:7; 56:1; Jer 22:15; Ezek 45:9.

3. Chris Marshall, *The Little Book of Biblical Justice: A Fresh Approach to the Bible's Teachings on Justice* (Intercourse, Pa.: Good Books, 2005), 10-21.

6. AVENGING BLOOD

1. Roland de Vaux, O.P., *Ancient Israel: Its Life and Institutions*, trans. John McHugh (1961; repr., Grand Rapids: Eerdmans, 1997), 20-23.

2. Ibid., 11.

3. D. J. F. de Quervain, U. Fischbacker, V. Treyer, M. Schellhammer, U. Schnyder, A. Buck, and E. Fehr, "The Neural Basis of Altruistic Punishment," *Science* 305, no. 5688 (August 27, 2004): 1254-58.

4. William Ian Miller, *Eye for An Eye* (Cambridge and New York: Cambridge University Press, 2006).

7. PROTECTING THE VULNERABLE

1. For the background here, I am indebted to Roya Hakakian, an Iranian woman who survived the 1979 Revolution, and who wrote an article entitled "Pray for Neda," http://www.cnn.com/2009/WORLD/meast/06/26/hakakian.neda/index.html.

2. María Pilar Aquino, *Our Cry for Life: Feminist Theology from Latin America,* trans. Dinah Livingstone (Maryknoll, N.Y.: Orbis Books, 1993), 103.

3. Exodus 3:7 is a turning point in the understanding of God's *hesed*—the divine loving-kindness that reaches into history to liberate and care for those in need.

4. John Dominic Crossan, *God and Empire: Jesus against Rome, Then and Now* (San Francisco: HarperSanFrancisco, 2007), 54. I draw several of the major themes in this section from pp. 50-54.

5. Alice Walker, *The Color Purple: A Novel* (New York: Harcourt Brace Jovanovich, 1982), 1.

6. *Fields of Mudan* (film, 2004), written and directed by Steven Chang [Stevo].

8. BEARING THE PAIN OF OTHERS

1. André Schwarz-Bart, *The Last of the Just,* trans. Stephen Becker (1960; repr., Cambridge, Mass.: R. Bentley, 1981).

2. An example of this approach is found in Regina M. Schwartz, *The Curse of Cain: The Violent Legacy of Monotheism* (Chicago: University of Chicago Press, 1997).

3. René Girard is one of the most creative thinkers of our time on the topic of human violence. See, for example, *Violence and the Sacred,* trans. Patrick Gregory (Baltimore: Johns Hopkins University Press, 1977); *Things Hidden since the Foundation of the World,* trans. Stephen Bann and Michael Metteer (Stanford, Calif.: Stanford University Press, 1987); and *I See Satan Fall like Lightning,* trans. James G. Williams (Maryknoll, N.Y.: Orbis Books, 2001).

4. Cf. Girard, *Things Hidden,* 210.

9. EMBODYING THE JUSTICE OF GOD

1. Juan Mateos, "The Message of Jesus," *Sojourners* 6, no. 8 (July 1977): 8-16.

2. In reality, this combined text from Isaiah would not have been found in a synagogue scroll. The author of Luke apparently combines passages from Isa 61:1-2 and Isa 58:6 to focus his vision of Jesus as servant of God and the fulfillment of the ancient dream of solidarity for the poor.

3. Marcus Borg, *Meeting Jesus Again for the First Time: The Historical Jesus and the Heart of Contemporary Faith* (San Francisco: HarperSanFrancisco, 1994), 52.

10. Proclaiming the Kingdom of God

1. Oscar Romero, *Through the Year with Oscar Romero: Daily Meditations*, trans. Irene B. Hodgson (Cincinnati: St. Anthony Messenger Press, 2005), 165.

2. See especially Johannes Baptist Metz, *Faith in History and Society: Toward a Practical Fundamental Theology*, trans. David Smith (New York: Seabury, 1980); and *A Passion for God: The Mystical-Political Dimension of Christianity*, trans. J. Matthew Ashley (New York, Paulist, 1998).

3. For a more thorough treatment of the biblical background, see Albert Nolan, *Jesus before Christianity* (Maryknoll, N.Y.: Orbis Books, 1978), especially 10-19, 92-100.

4. John Dominic Crossan provides credible evidence to call them "urban terrorists," since they tended to murder high-profile Roman collaborators in the midst of large crowds during the Jewish festivals; see *God and Empire: Jesus against Rome, Then and Now* (San Francisco: HarperSanFrancisco, 2007), 89-91.

5. Roberto S. Goizueta, "From Calvary to Galilee," *America*, vol. 194, no. 14, April 17, 2006, 14-15.

11. Living in Solidarity

1. John Dominic Crossan, *God and Empire: Jesus against Rome, Then and Now* (San Francisco: HarperSanFrancisco, 2007), 15-29.

2. Ibid., 31-45.

3. Elisabeth Schüssler Fiorenza, *In Memory of Her: A Feminist Theological Reconstruction of Christian Origins* (New York: Crossroad, 1983), 205ff.

4. Marcus Borg and John Dominic Crossan, *The First Paul: Reclaiming the Radical Visionary behind the Church's Conservative Icon* (New York: HarperOne, 2009).

5. Ibid., 47.

6. Ibid., 114-15.

12. Creating the Beloved Community

1. Martin Luther King, Jr., *Where Do We Go from Here: Chaos or Community* (New York: Harper & Row, 1967), 9.
2. Martin Luther King, Jr., *Strength to Love* (New York: Harper & Row, 1961), 64.
3. Pope Benedict XVI, *Caritas in Veritate*, encyclical letter on Integral Human Development in Charity and Truth (Vatican City: Libreria Editrice Vaticana, 2009), #1.

13. Moving beyond Armageddon

1. Hal Lindsey, *The Late Great Planet Earth* (Grand Rapids: Zondervan, 1970).
2. Barbara R. Rossing, *The Rapture Exposed: The Message of Hope in the Book of Revelation* (Boulder, Colo.: Westview, 2004), 4.
3. As quoted in Jane Lampman, "The End of the World," *Christian Science Monitor*, February 18, 2004.
4. This term was made famous by the late Robert McNamara, former U.S. Secretary of Defense.

14. Pursuing Peace

1. *Gaudium et Spes* (The Pastoral Constitution on the Church in the Modern World), in *Vatican Council II: Constitutions, Decrees, and Declarations*, ed. Austin Flannery, O.P. (Northport, N.Y.: Costello, 1996), #39, paragraph 2; also quoted in the *Catechism of the Catholic Church*, #1049.
2. James W. Douglass, *The Nonviolent Coming of God* (Maryknoll, N.Y.: Orbis Books, 1991; repr., Eugene, Ore.: Wipf & Stock, 2006).
3. Walter Wink, *The Human Being: Jesus and the Enigma of the Son of Man* (Minneapolis: Fortress, 2002), xi.
4. Douglass, *Nonviolent Coming of God*, 45.
5. John Dominic Crossan, *God and Empire: Jesus against Rome, Then and Now* (San Francisco: HarperSanFrancisco, 1007), 211.

Selected Bibliography

Aquino, María Pilar. *Our Cry for Life: Feminist Theology from Latin America*. Translated by Dinah Livingstone. Maryknoll, N.Y.: Orbis Books, 1993.

Armstrong, Karen. *A History of God: The 4,000-Year Quest of Judaism, Christianity, and Islam*. New York: Alfred A. Knopf, 1993.

————. *The Great Transformation: The Beginning of Our Religious Traditions*. New York: Alfred A. Knopf, 2006.

————. *Islam: A Short History*. New York: Alfred A. Knopf, 1993.

Auden, W. H. *Collected Poems*. Edited by Edward Mendelson. New York: Random House, 1976.

Benedict XVI. *Caritas in Veritate*. Encyclical letter on Integral Human Development in Charity and Truth. Vatican City: Libreria Editrice Vaticana, 2009.

Borg, Marcus. *Meeting Jesus Again for the First Time: The Historical Jesus and the Heart of Contemporary Faith*. San Francisco: HarperSanFrancisco, 1994.

Borg, Marcus, and John Dominic Crossan. *The First Paul: Reclaiming the Radical Visionary behind the Church's Conservative Icon*. New York: HarperOne, 2009.

Brueggemann, Walter. *The Prophetic Imagination*. Philadelphia: Fortress, 1978.

Buber, Martin. *I and Thou*. Translated by Walter Kaufmann. 1970. Reprint, New York: Scribner, 1996.

Camara, Helder. *The Spiral of Violence*. Translated by Della Couling. Denville, N.J.: Dimension Books, 1971.

Campbell, Joseph. *The Inner Reaches of Outer Space: Metaphor as Myth and as Religion*. New York: A. van der Marck, 1986.

Crossan, John Dominic. *God and Empire: Jesus against Rome, Then and Now*. San Francisco: HarperSanFrancisco, 2007.

Douglass, James W. *The Nonviolent Coming of God*. Maryknoll, N.Y.: Orbis Books, 1991. Reprint, Eugene, Ore.: Wipf & Stock, 2006.

————. *The Non-Violent Cross: A Theology of Revolution and Peace.* New York: Macmillan, 1968.

Eiseley, Loren C. *The Immense Journey: An Imaginative Naturalist Explores the Mysteries of Man and Nature.* New York: Random House, 1956.

Flannery, Austin, O.P., ed. *Vatican Council II: Constitutions, Decrees, and Declarations.* Northport, N.Y.: Costello, 1996.

Girard, René. *I See Satan Fall like Lightning.* Translated by James G. Williams. Maryknoll, N.Y.: Orbis Books, 2001.

————. *Things Hidden since the Foundation of the World.* Translated by Stephen Bann and Michael Metteer. Stanford, Calif.: Stanford University Press, 1987.

————. *Violence and the Sacred.* Translated by Patrick Gregory. Baltimore: Johns Hopkins University Press, 1977.

Hardt, Michael, and Antonio Negri. *Empire.* Cambridge, Mass.: Harvard University Press, 2000.

Haught, John F. *Deeper than Darwin: The Prospect of Religion in the Age of Evolution.* Boulder, Colo: Westview, 2003.

————. *God after Darwin: A Theology of Evolution.* 2nd ed. Boulder, Colo.: Westview, 2008.

Jäger, Willigis. *Search for the Meaning of Life: Essays and Reflections on the Mystical Experience.* Liguori, Mo.: Triumph Books, 1995.

Johnson, Elizabeth A. *Quest for the Living God: Mapping Frontiers in the Theology of God.* New York: Continuum, 2007.

Kennedy, Eugene C. *The Now and Future Church: The Psychology of Being an American Catholic.* Garden City, N.Y.: Doubleday, 1984.

King, Martin Luther, Jr. *Strength to Love.* New York: Harper & Row, 1961.

————. *Where Do We Go from Here: Chaos or Community?* New York: Harper & Row, 1967.

Kristof, Nicholas D., and Sheryl WuDunn. *Half the Sky: Turning Oppression into Opportunity for Women Worldwide.* New York: Alfred A. Knopf, 2009.

Lawrence, Bruce B. *Shattering the Myth: Islam beyond Violence.* 1998. Reprint, Princeton, N.J.: Princeton University Press, 2006.

Lindsey, Hal. *The Late Great Planet Earth.* Grand Rapids: Zondervan, 1970.

Marshall, Chris. *The Little Book of Biblical Justice: A Fresh Approach to the Bible's Teachings on Justice.* Intercourse, Pa.: Good Books, 2005.

Metz, Johannes Baptist. *Faith in History and Society: Toward a Practical Fundamental Theology.* Translated by David Smith. New York: Seabury, 1980.

————. *A Passion for God: The Mystical-Political Dimension of Christianity.* Translated by J. Matthew Ashley. New York: Paulist, 1998.

Miles, Jack. *God: A Biography.* New York: Alfred A. Knopf, 1995.

Miller, William Ian. *Eye for An Eye.* Cambridge and New York: Cambridge University Press, 2006.

Mortenson, Greg. *Stones into Schools: Promoting Peace with Books, Not Bombs, in Afghanistan and Pakistan*. New York: Viking, 2009.

Mortenson, Greg, with David Oliver Relin. *Three Cups of Tea: One Man's Mission to Promote Peace—One School at a Time*. New York: Penguin Books, 2007.

Neihardt, John G. *Black Elk Speaks, Being the Life Story of a Holy Man of the Oglala Sioux as Told through John G. Neihardt*. 1932. Reprint, Lincoln: University of Nebraska Press, 1968.

Nolan, Albert. *Jesus before Christianity*. Maryknoll, N.Y.: Orbis Books, 1978.

Ó'Murchú, Diarmuid. *Ancestral Grace: Meeting God in Our Human Story*. Maryknoll, N.Y.: Orbis Books, 2008.

Phillips, J. B., trans. *The New Testament in Modern English*. New York: Macmillan, 1962.

Prunier, Gérard. *The Rwanda Crisis: History of Genocide*. New York: Columbia University Press, 1995.

Romero, Oscar. *Through the Year with Oscar Romero: Daily Meditations*. Translated by Irene B. Hodgson. Cincinnati: St. Anthony Messenger Press, 2005.

Rossing, Barbara R. *The Rapture Exposed: The Message of Hope in the Book of Revelation*. Boulder, Colo.: Westview, 2004.

Schüssler Fiorenza, Elisabeth. *In Memory of Her: A Feminist Theological Reconstruction of Christian Origins*. New York: Crossroad, 1983.

Schwarz-Bart, André. *The Last of the Just*. Translated by Stephen Becker. 1960. Reprint, Cambridge, Mass.: R. Bentley, 1981.

Swimme, Brian, and Thomas Berry. *The Universe Story: From the Primordial Flaring Forth to the Ecozoic Era—A Celebration of the Unfolding of the Cosmos*. San Francisco: HarperSanFrancisco, 1992.

Synod of Bishops, 1971. *Justice in the World*. Washington, D.C.: United States Conference of Catholic Bishops, 1972.

Teilhard de Chardin, Pierre. *The Future of Man*. Translated by Norman Denny. New York: Harper & Row, 1964.

Tolle, Eckhart. *A New Earth: Awakening to Your Life's Purpose*. New York: Dutton/Penguin, 2006.

Vaux, Roland de. *Ancient Israel: Its Life and Institutions*. Translated by John McHugh. 1961. Reprint, Grand Rapids: Eerdmans, 1997.

Walker, Alice. *The Color Purple: A Novel*. New York: Harcourt Brace Jovanovich, 1982.

Wiesel, Elie. *Night*. Translated by Stella Rodway. New York: Hill & Wang, 1960. Reprint, New York: Bantam, 1982.

Wink, Walter. *Engaging the Powers: Discernment and Resistance in a World of Domination*. Minneapolis: Fortress, 1992.

———. *Naming the Powers: The Language of Power in the New Testament*. Philadelphia: Fortress, 1984.

———. *The Powers That Be: Theology for a New Millennium.* New York: Doubleday, 1998.

———. *Unmasking the Powers: The Invisible Forces That Determine Human Existence.* Philadelphia: Fortress, 1986.

Wright, Robert. *The Evolution of God.* New York: Little, Brown, 2009.

Index